Praise

"This is a great business novel—both entertaining and thought-provoking. It brilliantly captures the problems and dilemmas that organizations are struggling with."

— **Christian Feldbech Nissen**, thought leader and management consultant, Denmark

"Just wow! I couldn't wait to read what happened next. The plot is unpredictable, but it also feels real and possible. The book is packed with amazing insights and ends in a place I didn't expect when I started reading. I love the way the characters develop—watching them change through Marie's perspective is a great ride."

— **Joe Auslander**, post-transformation dude, New Zealand

"This book will prepare you as a leader better than any training. A realistic story of people dealing with complex problems and communication issues, *Maneuvering Monday* gave me flashbacks from my time as a manager."

— **Dimitri Borisevich**, startup advisor, Denmark

maneuvering MONDAY

A story of driving transformation when your people push back and your leaders look away

ANNE KATRINE CARLSSON SEJR
IVANNA MIKHAILOVNA ROSENDAL

Rethink

First published in Great Britain in 2025
by Rethink Press (www.rethinkpress.com)

Cover images licensed by Ingram Image

Contents

Character map

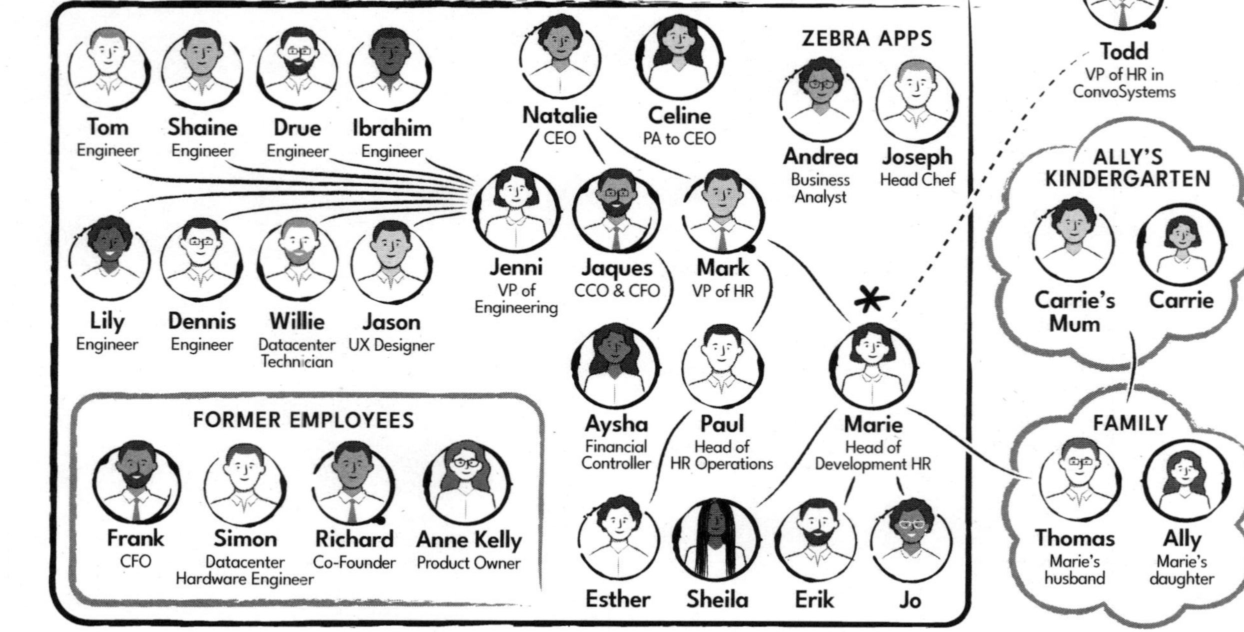

Preface

Have you ever read a business book outlining the "steps to business bliss" but found that reality doesn't quite align with the steps proposed? Perhaps you were annoyed by this disconnect? Then this book is for you.

This is a work of fiction, but it isn't a fable written to lead you to a certain conclusion. Rather, we describe a business and tell the story of the people that work there in a way that we hope feels real. We want you to draw your own conclusions, however they apply to you, and we hope you'll feel inspired to improve your place of work.

You'll get to follow characters who are attempting, to the best of their abilities, to change things for the better. They try, then fail. They learn. They change tactics. Sometimes they succeed. Sometimes they trust the wrong people. Not everything is in their control, and the outcomes are the sum of their efforts, not one person's master plan—just like work in the real world.

This is also how we wrote the book. We released the initial chapter drafts as podcast episodes, and we invited guest experts to comment on the story and advise the characters. Through this process, we got to know our own characters better and saw how they could act differently from the ways we'd anticipated. You can listen to the first draft of this story and the expert commentary at: https://maneuveringmonday.buzzsprout.com

The guest experts have shaped this book, as have our listeners and especially our beta readers, who were the first to read the book in its entirety. And we have written this book in partnership with each other: Ivanna wrote the story, and AK produced the podcast. We have both spent countless hours bringing the characters of this book to life and discussing the narrative arcs and podcast episode themes. During the creation of this book we changed jobs, had children, moved continents, bought houses, and fell in love. Our commitment to each other and our characters has remained steadfast throughout, because we believe that maneuvering work for the better has to be something we all do, regardless of our title or hierarchical position. Work occupies too much of our time to be a waste of time. Each of us can make it a little bit better.

Marie On A Mission

Marie poured herself a cup of coffee in the kitchenette while Jason waited for her in the conference room. The conference room was in the reception area, where they usually met with clients and external guests. It was late afternoon. Jason had asked Marie if she "had a minute" during lunch, and she'd suggested they talk while they ate. Jason had blushed, taken a couple of steps backward, and said he had a deadline. When Marie returned to her desk after lunch, she'd seen an invite from him for a meeting marked "Private." Her ten years in HR had given her a pretty good idea of what Jason had on his mind, especially so late in the month.

The coffee machine finished sputtering out Marie's latte. She brushed back her long, brown hair and straightened her glasses. She pulled down her skirt and took a deep breath. Then, she picked up her coffee cup and headed toward the conference room.

Marie sat across from Jason at the conference table. Jason was looking down, twisting his hands under the table.

"It helps when you have something to stir," Marie said. "Are you sure you don't want a drink?"

"No, let's get this over with," Jason said.

"Alright," said Marie, looking directly at him. "What's on your mind?"

"I've grown a lot here during the past three years," Jason started. "You took me in fresh from university. But I haven't been happy the past year," he continued, then paused. He took a breath and looked straight at Marie. "So, I will be leaving for a new job."

Marie felt her eyes moisten while she forced herself to keep smiling. Jason livened up and kept talking. "It's down the street, actually, and I'll get to do more of the work I've enjoyed doing here."

Marie's smile faded as she suddenly realized who was down the street. "You're leaving for the defense contractor?" she exclaimed. Jason nodded softly. "But you're a pacifist!" she said loudly, failing to reel in her emotions. "We've sent you to so many conferences to talk about the ethics of designing apps for children. Now you're going to design apps for war?"

There was a pause.

"In a way," Jason started, "conscript soldiers are also children."

Marie raised an eyebrow in disbelief. She managed to hold herself together for the remainder of the conversation with Jason, and they hugged when they parted ways.

Marie went straight to her office and closed the door. She sank into her armchair and remembered that her coffee mug was still on the conference room table, lukewarm and probably leaving a ring. "Fuck," she exclaimed in a half-whisper.

It was not the fact that Jason was leaving, specifically, even though Marie couldn't get her mind off what seemed like gaps in his reasoning. Soldiers as kids? It felt like baloney. She couldn't shake the inkling that Jason Wells, a twenty-seven-year-old UX designer passionate about ethical UI design for children, was so miserable at Zebra Apps that he would compromise one of his core beliefs to join a company he had morally sworn off previously.

This was the fourth resignation this March, with only one more day of the month remaining. Of a company of three hundred people, four people leaving in any given month was a lot. February had cost them seven people and January five. Core employees were leaving—people who had built the company and stuck it out during good times and bad. Right now, times were good for Zebra Apps. They had achieved double-digit growth in both revenue and number of employees. They had just secured a big implementation in Germany. They were hitting their KPIs and had given generous bonuses to all employees at the end of last year.

Marie's train of thought was interrupted by her phone ringing. Looking down at the display, she immediately swiped to pick up. It was her boss's boss, Natalie Jensen, the CEO of Zebra Apps. There was a rattling on the other end of the line.

"Hello?" Marie said.

"Ah, yes, hi Marie," said Natalie. The rattling continued. "Mark called earlier and said we've had three resignations this month." (Mark was the VP of HR and Marie's boss.)

"Actually, it's four now," Marie sighed.

"Four?" Natalie repeated, elevating her voice.

"Yes, I just spoke to Jason Wells. He's leaving, too."

"That is unfortunate," Natalie sighed. "He was supposed to give a keynote at that private school in Berlin next month."

"That's right," Marie gasped. The rattling started again, and Marie stared at her phone for clues as to what the sound was. Wrapping paper? Bubble wrap? It stopped.

"I'm curious about your take on why people are fleeing like rats off a sinking ship?" Natalie said, finally.

"I can't quite understand it. People I would never have imagined leaving are making unexpected employment choices," Marie said. "Take Jason," she continued, "he's going to work for the defense contractor down the road."

Natalie laughed out loud. "Guess he's going to have to change his X handle," she thundered, more playful than angry.

Marie smiled to herself. His handle was @pacifist_jason. "It feels to me like he's trying to get away from us more than he's interested in this opportunity," Marie said.

"Our employees are not thriving," Natalie said in a serious tone.

"I guess you're right," Marie nodded.

"Then that is an HR issue," Natalie concluded. "All yours to fix." The rattling began anew.

Marie suddenly understood where Natalie was going with this, her eyes widening. "Wait ..." she said.

"Aren't you the director of HR development?" Natalie asked rhetorically. "Aren't you responsible for developing us to be a good place to work?"

"Well, yes ..." Marie hesitated.

"Then this is your time to shine. I would like a plan from you by Wednesday on how to fix it."

"Alright ..." Marie said slowly.

"And if anyone else quits, just tell them no!" Natalie laughed and hung up.

Marie stared at her phone in disbelief. Then, a seed of hope rose in her stomach. If this was hers to fix, maybe it was fixable. What if she could reverse the flow of resignations? She stood up. What if they could still be a place where people wanted to work? After all, she had a PhD in organizational design. She had worked as a consultant at Business Consulting Group prior to joining Zebra and had done her fair share of organizational transformations.

Marie packed her bag. Wednesday was a week away, and she left the office for the first time in months with hope and a sense of mission.

It's Probably Not The Soda

Holding her daughter Ally's hand as she nodded off that night, Marie stared intently into the night light above her daughter's bed until a simple plan locked into place in her mind. She would find out why people were leaving. She would benchmark the employment terms of Zebra Apps against similar companies and analyze the data to determine the underlying factors that differentiated them from the competition. The conclusions could be summed up neatly on slides, convincing Mark and Natalie to support her proposed course of action. She rescheduled all her meetings for the next day to get a head start.

Arriving at the office the following day, Marie stopped by the conference room where she had met with Jason and picked up her coffee cup from the conference table. She put it in the sink in the kitchenette. She picked up a clean cloth from a drawer and ran it under the tap. She turned to head back to the conference room to wash the ring from the table, only to find Simon standing behind her.

"You're here early," Marie said.

"I was hoping you were in," Simon said, "but you weren't in your office."

"No," Marie said, looking at the cloth in her hand, "I had something I wanted to take care of first."

"Can we talk?" Simon said.

"Sure." Marie turned around to put the cloth down near the sink.

"We can go in here," said Simon, pointing to the same conference room where Marie had met with Jason.

As they sat down, Marie tried to ignore the ring on the table made by her cup. She sat next to it, diagonally across from Simon.

"I'm resigning," he said as Marie adjusted her chair to face him.

"Alright," Marie replied, trying to mask the annoyance in her voice.

Simon's smile contracted. "That's it?" he asked.

"I'm sorry, what?" she replied.

"That's your reaction? 'Alright,'" Simon made air quotes with his hands.

Marie remembered her plan from last night and decided to dig in. "Where are you heading?" Marie asked.

"Nowhere," Simon said, still smiling.

Marie waited for him to say more. He looked straight into her eyes but did not move.

"Are you planning on taking some time off?" Marie asked, knowing that she was walking straight into his trap.

"No, I'm not 'taking time off,'" Simon said, making air quotes again, this time with his arms stretched above his head.

Simon was a hardware engineer who had been integral to creating their data center. Now, he was in charge of it. He was not known for being likable but was popular with the other engineers for having no filter with management.

"Help me understand," Marie said.

Simon's smile widened, and he leaned back in his chair with his hands intertwined behind his neck. "Marie," he said, "you have no idea what's going on, do you?"

After the meeting, Marie hurried to her office. She slapped her notebook on her desk and sat down. Where to start? What Simon had said kept going through her head. She wrote down:

You have no idea what is going on.

Marie turned the page in her notebook and called Jason.

"I have a couple of follow-up questions from our conversation yesterday," Marie said.

"Would you say that your current salary is a major reason for you leaving?" Marie asked.

Jason was quiet. "No," he said, finally.

"Surely you will be making more in your new job?" Marie asked, surprised.

"No …" Jason said, "I'll be making less."

Now Marie was quiet. She suddenly remembered the coffee stain on the conference table. "Will you have better benefits like time off, free lunch, newer equipment, parking …?"

Jason cut in, "They have free soda."

"Free … soda?" Marie repeated.

"Yes," Jason said. "Otherwise, it's the same package."

"So, you're taking a pay cut and getting more or less the same perks, except for free soda," she concluded.

"Look," Jason started, "I don't want to get in trouble here."

"No, no," Marie assured him.

"I don't care about the perks," he said. "I care that I feel happy when I wake up in the morning. That my work counts." Jason stopped talking, but it seemed like he had more to say.

"Go on," Marie encouraged.

"We used to be a place like that," he said.

"What changed?" Marie asked.

"I don't want to go into details here. Is this conversation required?"

"No, I'm just trying to understand," Marie said.

"I think you should speak to Anne," Jason suggested.

They said their goodbyes and hung up. She couldn't believe that Jason didn't feel like his work counted. He had been the one to advocate that they employ UX principles carefully when developing apps for children—that they act responsibly to make sure that the design was engaging but not manipulative. Something didn't add up. She did not want to call Anne, so she browsed through her LinkedIn connections. Todd would be a good place to start. Todd was the VP of HR at ConvoSystems, a software development company that competed fiercely for engineers with Zebra Apps.

"Hey, Marie," Todd said.

"There's no sneaking up on you," Marie joked. Todd had clearly saved her number in his contacts.

"I need to keep my eye on you," he said. "Stealing away my employees."

They both laughed.

"Seems like the market is pretty fluid right now," Marie said. "People are changing jobs like crazy."

"To be honest, our engineer Shaine is the first person to leave us this year," Todd said. "*You've* broken our perfect record."

"Sorry about that," Marie said.

"I can't blame him," Todd said, "I heard that he's getting a big salary bump."

"About that," Marie started, "I wanted to compare our standard offerings against our peers—"

Todd cut in, "About time! You must be swimming in subscriptions over there with the offers you throw at my people. You're going to force us offshore."

With that, they reviewed the standard packages they were offering to different employee profiles.

She then called three other HR colleagues at companies similar to Zebra Apps. The fourth name Marie had her eye on from her LinkedIn contacts didn't respond, so she followed up with an email.

Marie's boss, Mark, walked into her office as she was closing off the last call. He was about to step out again, but she waved him in and pointed him to the armchair. He ran his hand through his dark blond hair and pulled up the pant legs of his dark gray, tailored suit as he sat down. He stretched his legs, almost reaching Marie's feet from across the room. She hung up and scribbled a note in her notebook before looking up.

"Simon, too?" Mark said. "What a joke."

"Joke?" she echoed, losing her train of thought.

"Now we don't have to fire that joker," he said, puffing out his chest.

"To my knowledge, no one was planning on firing him," Marie said. "Hardware engineers are hard to find."

"Well, you know …" he started.

"What do I know?" Marie said, losing all patience.

"You shouldn't be having these conversations," Mark said, his face now stern.

Marie looked at him with her eyebrows raised.

"People should be going straight to their line manager," Mark went on.

"What do you propose I do, Mark, send them away?" Marie said through her teeth.

"Send them to me," Mark said. "I'm the head of HR."

"Your office is right next to mine," Marie gestured. "Nothing is stopping people from opening your door."

"You're nice, so people come to you," Mark said. Marie looked straight at Mark's face. After a pause, he continued, "It's not even your job to listen to people quitting."

"Natalie just told me it's my job to *fix* that people are quitting," Marie said.

"She said that, huh?" he said. "Well …"

Without another word, he got up and went straight out the door, striking his hip on the doorframe but not stopping to acknowledge the pain.

Marie picked up her notebook and pointed it at the door as if to signal to the air left behind by Mark's departure that she had something else she wanted to tell him. She put the notebook down and rubbed her forehead with her hand. Her hand smelled like a stale washcloth. She went to the bathroom to wash the smell off.

Looking at herself in the bathroom mirror, she thought about Mark. Their relationship had not always been so strained. He was the one who hired her. They met through a professional network. She reached out to him after he gave a keynote about empowering specialists to deliver great results. She couldn't put a finger on the exact moment she stopped trusting him. After several years, she started noticing that he failed to make the hard choices to protect the principles he preached. No wonder his door was not the one people went through when they quit.

Wait a minute, she thought, *employees were picking her door, not only because they expected her to listen, but also because they expected her to act on what she heard.*

She dried her hands and went back to her office. She dialed Anne Kelly. The first name on her list. The last person she wanted to call. After seven rings, Marie hung up. Maybe Anne didn't want to talk to her either. She decided to start writing up the presentation for Mark and Natalie.

When she opened her laptop, the fourth HR contact had responded to her email, offering up their benchmarking data. Now, she had a complete overview of the offers from their key talent competitors. When the competition for technical specialists was so fierce, there was a sense of camaraderie between the recruiters. They worked together to lobby for universities to offer more technical studies and to have lower barriers to bringing in technical specialists from abroad. From her contacts, she learned that Zebra Apps was paying slightly above the market rate for software specialists, quite a bit above the rate for hardware specialists, and average for other functions. This was a clear indication that money was not the reason people were leaving. They were all offering similar packages for other benefits: employee lunches, free parking, pension schemes, healthcare benefits, flexible working arrangements, high-end equipment, and snacks. Three of the five companies she spoke to also offered free soda.

Marie put her notes together on three slides. She looked at her watch and saw that the canteen was about to close. She rushed out of her office, leaving her phone on her desk.

In The Past Year

In the canteen, Marie put orange sauce—the sorry leftovers of what used to be butter chicken—on some rice. The head chef popped his head out of the kitchen door and caught Marie's glance.

"I lost track of time today," she explained.

The chef laughed.

"Don't you worry; we're hiring additional kitchen staff this month to keep up," he said. "Mark shared your hiring projections for the coming year. Phew!" He gestured an upward-growing curve with his hand.

"Yeah, we're growing," Marie said. *If only we could keep the people we already have*, Marie thought, *growth would be easier to sustain.*

At that moment, Natalie rushed in, picked up a plate, and grabbed three slices of bread. She walked over and sat across from Marie. "Slim pickings," she said, taking a big bite of bread.

Marie nodded.

"I heard you spoke to Mark today," Natalie went on, already on her final piece of bread.

"Yeah, he came by my office," said Marie.

"Look, his pride was hurt," Natalie said.

Marie looked at her, tilting her head in disbelief. "His pride?" Marie repeated.

"You told him I asked you to fix the retention problem," Natalie said.

"Yes," Marie said.

"Now, you and I know that Mark is not a fixer," Natalie continued, "but let's not make him feel threatened."

"Am I making him feel threatened?" Marie said.

"Just don't rub his nose in it," Natalie concluded.

Before Marie could respond, Natalie got up to leave without glancing back.

Marie clenched her jaw. The only thing that matters is figuring out why people are leaving, she thought. *That is within my control,* she told herself, her jaw relaxing.

She decided to stop by Natalie's office on the way back from lunch to share her preliminary results. Natalie's door was closed. Marie glanced through the glass next to the door and saw Mark inside. Natalie waved her in.

"Great, you're both here," Marie started, wanting to be inclusive toward Mark. "I wanted to show you my initial findings."

"You have findings already?" Mark said, surprised.

"I spent the day benchmarking us against our competitors," she said.

Marie pulled up the presentation and took Mark and Natalie through the slides.

"So, we pay our people too much," Natalie said with a big smile.

"Free soda," Mark said, writing in his notebook.

"It's probably not the soda ..." Marie remarked. She was about to continue but caught Natalie looking at her. Natalie shook her head almost imperceptibly. Marie stopped talking, leaving her sentence hanging.

"This doesn't explain why people are leaving," Natalie said. "This explains why people should be staying."

Marie blushed. Natalie was right. This concluded nothing.

"Have you looked at the exit interview reports?" Mark asked.

"No, I wasn't aware that we documented exit interviews," Marie said.

"If people came to me, I could follow the process," Mark said.

Why are you the only one who knows about this process? Marie thought but said instead, "Would you be willing to share them with me?"

Natalie nodded approvingly at Marie.

Mark promised to send Marie a link to the files. After she exited Natalie's office, she felt dizzy walking down the hallway. But she couldn't quite pin down the origin of her emotional vertigo.

Back in her office, Esther, the benefits manager, knocked on her door. Esther was hugging a stack of papers with both hands.

"I've got your printouts for you," Esther said.

"My printouts?" Marie asked, raising an eyebrow.

"Mark said you wanted prints of exit interviews from the past year," Esther said.

As Esther was about to leave, Marie asked, "Do you know where these files are located on our drive?"

"Sure, I just printed them," Esther said, pointing to the stack. She showed Marie the location of the files in their HR folder. "See, there," Esther said, "arranged by month."

"Is Mark the only one who documents these?" Marie asked.

"He doesn't document them," Esther scoffed. "It's either me or Paul."

"But Paul is head of HR operations," Marie interjected. "I just mean that it would make more sense that someone from my team does this," she tried to explain.

"I have no interest in writing down people's complaints," Esther said, shaking her head.

Marie looked at Esther, trying to understand why Mark would want their benefits specialist to fill out exit interview forms.

"Anyway, I've got to go," Esther said. "Mark asked me to look into the taxation of free soda."

"What …" Marie opened her mouth, but Esther was already heading out the door.

Marie raised her arms up halfway and grunted in frustration. Then she saw the stack of paper on her desk and pulled it toward her. Under the stack of forms, Marie noticed her phone. It had five unanswered calls, all from Anne.

Before calling Anne back, Marie decided to look through her exit interview—for context, of course, and not to put off returning her call. She leafed through the forms. March, February, January … Anne resigned what seemed like an eternity ago. There it was—May. Not even a full year ago. She leafed to the "Reason for leaving" section. It said:

> "In the past year, Zebra Apps has changed dramatically. It used to be a company with principles and employees who were willing to go the extra mile to get things done. Now, we are employing Excel-sheet types and peacocks who do not contribute any real value to the company. The day that ASLO was declined for compassionate use was the day I knew I could no longer stay."

Marie thought back to the ASLO incident. Then she leafed through the stack of papers again. She found Jason's interview, conducted just today by Esther. She started reading the "Reason for leaving" section. It began:

> "In the past year, Zebra Apps stopped being the company I was hired to work for."

Marie stopped reading. In the past year? She glanced through the files from the full year, circling "in the past year" in more than three-fifths of the interviews. Marie looked out the window. It was dark outside, approaching 7:30 p.m. She yawned and picked up her bag. Walking out of the office, she looked back at her stack of exit interviews. *What has happened in the past year?* she asked herself. Right then, she remembered the coffee stain in the conference room. *The cleaners have probably washed that off by now,* she thought. *It's fine.* She nodded as if to convince herself.

Peace Over Pacifism

Anne was the original creator of ASLO. It was over six years old but had only reached product-market fit once the pandemic made classroom teaching impossible. Developed to support asynchronous learning in schools, it was the key to Zebra Apps' rapid expansion in recent years. Not only did it become a popular tool during lockdown, but they also found themselves riding on a paradigm shift in teaching methods. Teachers as instructors were on the way out and teachers as coaches and facilitators were on the way in. ASLO helped teachers curate content to be consumed as homework and supported in-class interaction by providing teachers with dashboards of students' progress. Powered by their AI algorithm, it even offered suggestions for teachers on how to help students progress. This AI was their most prized intellectual property and the reason they had strategically chosen to expand into hardware and build their own data center. It was part of their commitment to ethical software development. "Children's brains are not for commercial gain" was the slogan Jason used to finish his presentations with.

"This is the part that I don't get," Marie said to her husband, Thomas, while holding her toothbrush. "Anne was the most successful product developer at Zebra. Why would she leave just because of a disagreement?"

"I don't know," Thomas mumbled, not because he was disinterested but because he was brushing his teeth.

"ASLO is a huge success. If something I created became the most important product in my company, I would stay to see how it panned out," Marie added.

Thomas was drying his face with a towel. "It depends on what's important to you," he said. "Success may not mean material success." He whacked Marie playfully with the wet towel. "You're the one working in HR," he said. "You should know these things."

"Oh, your cheek!" Marie laughed and grabbed the towel out of his hands.

Thomas came in closer and put his arm around Marie. "Why are you obsessing over her? Come on, let's get some rest," he said.

On Fridays, Marie was the one to drop their daughter off at kindergarten. On the way, she would pass a drive-through bakery and pick up cinnamon buns for her team. When she entered the kitchenette downstairs that Friday, everyone from her team was already there. Marie put the brown bag on the kitchen island, and Sheila tore it open while continuing her story. Sheila had been on Marie's team for the past two years. Marie loved how she could get mid-level leaders and staff engaged in any training session with her contagious energy.

When she finished her story, Sheila looked at Marie. "Where were you all day yesterday?" she asked.

"I went down a rabbit hole," Marie said, "trying to figure out why people are leaving."

Sheila nodded.

"Hey, did you know about the exit interviews that Paul and Esther document?" Marie asked.

"Esther mentioned those to me," Sheila said. "She's not a fan."

"I'll need to talk to Mark about those," Marie said.

"So, why are people leaving?" Eric chimed in. Eric was the most senior member of Marie's team. He had been the head of Development HR at Sailtech prior to joining Zebra. At Zebra, he focused mainly on leadership development programs.

"Not because of salary or benefits," Marie said.

"We pay top of the market," Sheila confirmed.

"Yeah, I verified with my network," Marie said. "Except for free soda, we're on par or above our competitors."

"Probably not the soda," Eric chuckled.

"I read through recent exit interviews," Marie continued, "and found that three-fifths mentioned that they were leaving because we've changed in the past year."

"What happened in the past year?" Jo asked. Jo ran the project management competency development at Zebra Apps. She had been a successful project manager herself, but had since specialized in training others on how to develop the personal maturity and tools necessary to succeed.

"You tell me," Marie said. "I've been thinking about it since last night."

"Berlin is happening," Sheila said.

"ASLO is in 70% of schools," Eric said.

"The pandemic ended," Jo continued.

"We've grown by a third," Marie offered.

"Anne quit," Eric said. He looked at Marie. "Have you spoken to her?" he asked.

"She called me yesterday," Marie answered. "I need to call her back."

Eric nodded.

"We've hired a sales team," Sheila said, "and new managers."

Marie looked at Sheila. She was right. They had grown by a third, but the third was a new branch of their business. The development team was more or less intact—they had only replaced the people who left, not added new members.

"We've also got the new strategy," Eric said, interrupting Marie's train of thought.

"It's all about growth now," Jo sighed.

Marie nodded and took a bite of her cinnamon bun. Fridays were her favorite. She loved her team and enjoyed hearing their stories from the week gone by. Surrounded by them, she felt at ease. When she started at Zebra Apps, the entire HR organization used to meet up on Fridays together, but Paul, the head of HR operations, had concluded that Friday breakfast was too clichéd for an HR function, and soon only Marie's team showed up.

Back in her office, Marie made a note of what her team had said on the whiteboard:

New managers hired
Sales team
Berlin
New strategy
Growth
ASLO

She thought back to the ASLO incident with Anne. Anne had strongly suggested that they offer ASLO for free to all of Ukraine. Using ASLO, it did not matter if the teachers and students were displaced. They could continue their curriculum where they had left off. No generation of children would need to experience the education gap, as had happened during the Yugoslav Wars in the 1990s. It would have taken all the spare capacity in their data center to provide this service. And who knew for how long? Natalie would have none of it.

Suddenly, it dawned on Marie that they still had spare capacity in their data center that they did not know how to use. That was the whole purpose of the business case that Simon had been working on with Andrea, their business analyst. She took her phone from her coat pocket and called Simon.

"Hey Marie," Simon said, "you know I won't be keeping this number."

"The spare capacity in our data center—how much do we have?" she asked.

"Well, hello to you too," Simon said. "Is Natalie pounding that business case again?"

"No … I …" Marie said, looking at the whiteboard and lowering her voice, "How much capacity would we have needed to provide ASLO to Ukraine?"

Simon went quiet for a minute. "It would have been more than enough," he said.

"So …" Marie hesitated.

"So, it's a load of bullshit," Simon concluded.

Marie didn't know what to say next.

"Have you spoken to Anne?" Simon asked.

"Why does everyone want me to speak to Anne so badly?" Marie muttered.

"Well, you can keep going in circles if you prefer," Simon said.

"Have you seen Jason's new X handle?" Marie asked, changing the subject.

"I was the one who suggested it," Simon said with a chuckle. "@warandpeacejason is a nice bridge to his new career."

"How does that happen? How does someone just change their beliefs?" Marie said, suddenly wondering why she was asking Simon this.

"War happened," Simon said.

Marie nodded into her phone.

"You know his girlfriend's family is from Ukraine?" Simon added.

"No, I didn't know," Marie said.

"He was the one who suggested to Anne that we should offer up ASLO," Simon said.

"But we didn't," Marie said.

"No, we didn't want to inhibit our 'growth,'" Simon said, and Marie could feel him gesturing air quotes.

"What about you? Are you joining the army?" Marie joked.

"I really am leaving because I can't take it anymore," Simon said.

"And what is it that you can't take?" Marie asked.

"The hypocrisy, the bureaucracy, the processes," Simon answered but went quiet. "I just don't feel like we're on the same team anymore," he continued.

They spoke for a couple more minutes. When they hung up, Marie added "not same team" to her whiteboard. She felt warm inside after speaking to Simon, and it was not her usual rising anger. Jason's choice made sense now. Jason was a pacifist when he joined the company. When the war in Ukraine broke out, he cared more about keeping his family safe than he did about being a pacifist.

Marie heard footsteps approaching her open door. She looked up to find Mark stepping into her office.

"What's all this?" he asked, pointing at the two stacks of exit interviews on the table.

Marie rolled her eyes. "You told Esther to print the exit interviews instead of sending me the link," she almost shouted.

Mark considered her statement for a minute. Then he said quietly, "Marie, that's not true. I asked Esther to send you the link."

Marie looked at him, baffled. "Why didn't you just send me the link?" she asked.

"I haven't done an exit interview in months," he said. "Esther does this all the time."

He walked over to the whiteboard and looked at Marie's notes. "So, it's our culture," he said.

"Our culture?" Marie said.

"Not same team," he read, "adding on lots of new people, growing fast."

Marie looked at him in bewilderment. Then, she said, "You're right."

"Well, that's an easy fix," he said.

Marie couldn't tell if he was being sarcastic or sincere. "I've got to make a call," she said.

"Alright," he said, "well done."

He smiled at her, turned around, and went out the door. Marie had the same bad feeling in her gut as she always had after speaking with Mark. He said the right things. But, somehow, she always felt off balance after speaking with him. Left wondering. Feeling insane.

Too Many Meetings

At the lunch buffet, Marie was circling empty bowls of food. The chef emerged from the kitchen.

"I have something for you," he said. A few seconds later, he opened the door and presented Marie with a fully arranged plate.

"Whoa," Marie said.

"Saved some for you," said the chef.

Marie looked at him and felt her eyes tearing up. "Thank you," she said.

"Bon appétit," he said.

Marie was on her last bite when Jenni sat across from her. Jenni was the CTO of the company and headed up engineering. Before Jenni, no one person was in charge of technology. That used to make sense when Zebra only hired technologists and a couple of internal staff members, but things had changed. Jenni had been Anne's boss.

"Do you know what Anne is up to these days?" Marie asked.

"I haven't spoken to her since she left," Jenni said.

Marie shrugged.

"I heard that she's a consultant now," Jenni added.

"Oh," Marie said, genuinely surprised.

"It makes a lot of sense, really. She never cared about the technology anyway," Jenni went on.

"But she was the one who created some of our most successful products. She invented ASLO," Marie said, then forcefully closed her mouth to keep herself from saying more.

"She was in meetings all day long," Jenni went on.

"What kind of meetings?" Marie asked.

"She spoke to everyone. All the developers, all the engineers, everyone."

Marie digested the information. "What did she speak to them about?" she asked.

"That's the big question," Jenni said. "She didn't believe in 'reporting up.'" Jenni made air quotes with her fingers, still holding her fork in one hand.

Marie had a hard time reconciling this bit of information with what she knew about Anne. How everyone loved working with her. "What kind of consulting does she do now?" Marie asked.

"How to talk to people," Jenni said with a grin.

When Marie returned to her office, she googled Anne Kelly. There was a website now: annekelly.com. Jenni was right; Anne was a consultant. Marie read the "offerings" page. She felt uneasy. Why would Anne, their star product manager, become an HR consultant? Marie dialed Anne's number. It rang three times before Anne picked up.

"Hi Anne," Marie said, "is this a bad time?"

"I'm about to give a keynote," Anne said, "but I would like to speak to you."

"I can call you later," Marie suggested.

"I would prefer to meet," Anne said. "How about we meet in the coffee shop across the street from Zebra at 4:30 p.m.?"

"That should work, but I do have a hard stop at 5:30 p.m.," Marie said.

"We'll make it work. See you then," Anne said and hung up.

Make it work? Marie thought. *What was on Anne's agenda that may not fit into a whole hour?*

A Whole Hour

Marie decided to pack up her things and leave for the coffee shop early. She sat at a table in the corner, giving her a view of the entire intersection in front of the coffee shop. Traffic was picking up as people headed home early for the weekend.

She noticed a figure in a fuchsia power suit approaching the coffee shop. Looking closer, she realized it was Anne. Anne had usually worn the classic developer uniform while at Zebra Apps—a T-shirt with witty print and jeans or slacks. Marie checked her watch. It was only 3:55 p.m. They were both more than half an hour early.

Anne went straight to the counter to order, not noticing Marie in the corner. She exchanged a laugh with the barista. While Anne waited for her drink, she turned around and took a little step back as she noticed Marie. Anne nodded in Marie's direction and headed toward her table.

"We're both early," Marie smiled.

"Yes," Anne said, "I must admit, I snuck out early from the conference. I thought I would take a couple of minutes to get my thoughts together before we met."

"That was exactly my plan," Marie smiled.

"We can sit at separate tables and ignore each other for half an hour," Anne suggested with a straight face. Marie wasn't sure if Anne was making a joke or was serious but didn't want to risk being rude.

"No, no," Marie said, "this is just an informal conversation."

"Suit yourself." Anne sat down across from Marie, blocking her view of the street. Suddenly, Marie felt uneasy. Looking out on the street had provided a sort of comfort.

"So ..." Marie started.

"So, you haven't been picking up my calls," Anne said.

"You didn't pick up either," Marie said, surprising herself with her defensive attitude.

"That was one time," Anne said. "You didn't call me back after multiple attempts to reach you."

Marie was taken aback by Anne's confrontational words but decided to lean in. "I didn't want to speak to you," she said.

"I don't blame you," Anne said.

They sat in silence for a couple of minutes. Anne poured tea from her pot and smiled as she lifted her cup to smell the tea. "Oolong," Anne said.

"I never cared for that kind of tea," Marie said.

"It tastes a bit like camel," Anne said.

They both laughed.

Marie felt her shoulders lowering. She hadn't realized how tense she was. She sipped her cappuccino and looked at Anne. "You left quite a gap when you left," Marie said. "You're missed."

Anne looked straight at Marie. "I was holding engineering together."

Marie nodded.

"The system is insufficient if one person holds it all together," Anne said.

Marie rolled her eyes. "You always talk about systems," Marie said, "but people make up systems."

"People ultimately fail if the system isn't suitable for people," Anne said. "Like your department."

"What about my department?" Marie said, surprised.

"You hold HR together," Anne said.

"I guess I do," Marie said, having a hard time keeping back a smile.

"Face it," Anne said, "Mark isn't pulling his weight, Paul is disengaged, Esther is angry, and it's a miracle people get paid on time."

"What?" Marie said. She felt herself grab onto the side of the table as if it would provide her with support.

"Do you disagree?" Anne asked.

Marie let go of the table and put her hands in her lap.

"Is Mark pulling his weight?" Anne asked, eyes wide as she leaned forward.

"Well …" Marie didn't really want to answer that. She tried to find a redeeming quality of Mark's to mention.

"He did suggest that our culture is the problem," Marie said.

"And how did he reach that clever synthesis of the problem?" Anne asked, joining her fingertips into a diamond shape.

"He looked at the notes on my whiteboard," Marie said, suddenly feeling played again.

"You collected the data, wrote it up on your board, and Mark swooped in and stole the conclusion seconds before you had that exact same 'aha' moment?" Anne said, "What a hero indeed."

Marie bit her bottom lip and clenched her fists in front of her. "Paul isn't disengaged," Marie said, trying to change the course of the conversation.

"Paul is a good man," Anne said, "and you didn't give him a chance to get his feet under his desk when he was onboarded to lead HR operations."

"Me?" Marie said, leaning toward the table and holding her arm over her chest.

"The minute he entered the door, you got in his business," Anne said.

"What are you talking about?" Marie gasped as she sat back in her chair. She was starting to feel dizzy.

"You keep HR together. You step in. You see people and what they need. But by stepping in, you crowd Paul's initiative out. Just like Mark does, you swoop in before Paul has a chance to arrive at his own conclusions."

Marie wanted to respond. She wanted to fight.

Anne looked at Marie and smiled. "You see so much, yet you miss the whole picture," she said.

Marie clenched her fists. "And you see the whole picture, Miss HR consultant?" Marie said.

Anne chuckled. "HR consultant? Is that what I am?"

"You advise organizations on building teams," Marie said. "That is essentially what my team does at Zebra. It's HR."

"Your team," Anne said, "has essentially created a subculture in the organization. You have your own rules. For God's sake, you have your own breakfast."

"What's wrong with having a team breakfast?" Marie said.

"You stay out of the actual business," Anne said. "It's as if you're HR consultants who incidentally are on full-time contracts with Zebra."

"We're facilitators and coaches," Marie said. "We're supposed to stay out of the business."

"That's an excuse," Anne said. "You should be taking part. You should be engaging and challenging. You can change the system—a system that your colleagues are drowning in."

"Now, wait a minute—" Marie tried to interject.

"People are drowning, and you're staying on the sidelines trying to teach them how to swim. You need to drain the pool," Anne said.

Marie could feel anger rising. "Are you accusing me of not engaging? What about Andrea?" Marie said a bit louder than intended.

"Who's Andrea?" Anne asked quietly.

Marie smiled calmly. Now was her chance to put Anne in her place. "Andrea. The business analyst who was working with Simon on creating a business case for selling our excess hosting capacity," Marie said.

"That damn thing!" Anne said. "But wasn't the business analyst called Andy? He worked with Simon on that case."

"She prefers she/her pronouns. And her name is Andrea," Marie said, smiling intensely and waiting for Anne to react.

Anne sat back in her chair and scratched the side of her head for a minute. "I didn't know that," she said.

"Oh, you who know everyone and spend all your time talking to people in meetings," Marie said with a sarcastic tone. "You let poor Andrea squirm like a fish trying to get that information out of Simon while she was undergoing one of the biggest transitions in her life."

"Marie, I had no idea," Anne said, looking genuinely shocked.

"You're telling me I don't engage," Marie went on. "I was the one who protected her from that whole nonsense. I was the one who found her crying in the bathroom after Simon sent her on yet another figure-finding wild-goose chase just so that you could get back at management for not supporting your Ukraine idea for ASLO."

"Marie, I'm sorry, I really didn't know," Anne said.

"That's your problem right there," Marie said. "You think you're better than us. You're trying to tell me that I'm doing the wrong thing. It's actually you who is disengaged. You left the company, for crying out loud. You left just because things didn't go your way. Just because you didn't get to use a huge portion of company assets for purposes that wouldn't create any revenue. You left Jason to fend for himself."

"That's not fair," Anne said, looking down at the table. "I left because of Jason. I left because no matter how much I supported him and everyone in the rest of engineering, no one was supporting me."

"I always had your back," Marie said.

They sat in silence for a while. Marie tried to look past Anne out into the street. The intersection was packed with cars now.

"Why were you in meetings all the time?" Marie asked.

"What?" Anne asked, letting out a snicker.

"That's what Jenni said," Marie recalled, "that you weren't interested in the technology and were unavailable to her."

"Technology is easy," Anne said. "Creating an organizational system where people create great technology is hard. Especially for complex systems such as ASLO that stretch the limits of what's possible. That's why I was in meetings all day. Listening to the team and brokering."

"So, you were, in effect, managing the team," Marie concluded, "not Jenni."

"No, I was managing their creative energy," Anne said. "I was watching out for how we created as an ensemble."

"Ensemble? Were you putting on a theater show?" Marie snickered.

Anne looked at her with a straight face. "An ensemble is different from a team," Anne said. "It bends and adjusts depending on the people in the ensemble. It's more like an organism."

"You've given up on technology altogether, then?" Marie said. "As a career?"

"No … maybe. I just realized that it wasn't my key contribution," Anne said.

"Why didn't you come to me when you were creating your ensemble?" Marie asked.

"So you could do teamwork exercises with us?" Anne said with a huff.

Marie frowned.

"Don't take it the wrong way," Anne said, "but we needed continuous work on how we showed up for each other. A workshop wouldn't cut it."

Marie looked at her watch. It was 5:20 p.m. She looked at Anne. "It's already been an hour and a half," Marie said.

Anne looked at her. "Conversations take time," Anne replied. "Humans process things slower than machines. We process things emotionally and intellectually. The emotional part especially takes a toll."

Marie wasn't really listening. She was thinking of the question she really wanted to know the answer to. "Could we have offered ASLO to the displaced students and teachers of Ukraine?" Marie asked.

"We could have done that without any real cost to the company," Anne said.

"Why didn't we?" Marie asked.

"It's funny that you're asking me that," Anne said. "You should be asking Natalie."

"I have asked Natalie," Marie said. Marie looked at Anne. She couldn't quite figure out whether to trust her or not. "Something doesn't add up," Marie said after a pause.

Anne nodded but didn't say anything in reply. "It wasn't because I didn't get my way with ASLO that I left," Anne finally said. "Jason, Simon, and I would have spent our free time setting it up. We could have used the servers that we'd already installed anticipating expansion but hadn't yet allocated to paying subscribers. I'm pretty sure we could even have gotten funding from charities and government agencies to fund the subscription cost."

Marie could see that Anne was tearing up.

"We even created a damn business case for Natalie with pledges of support from donors and a plan for making it happen," Anne said, "but she and the new guy, the VP of sales, wouldn't hear it."

"We have become much more commercially focused," Marie said.

Anne was about to say more, but Marie looked at her watch again and saw it was 5:40 p.m. She almost jumped out of her seat and started packing her bag. "I'm sorry, but I have to go. My kid's kindergarten is having a flower party, and I'm on the planning committee," Marie said.

A Culture Program

On Sunday morning, Marie sat at her kitchen table, still in her pajamas. Her husband was outside pushing their daughter Ally on the swing. Marie drank a cup of coffee and scrolled through her LinkedIn feed on her phone. Another promotion. A quote from a business book accompanied by a personal story. Marie looked out the window to see Ally jumping off the swing and heading for the slide. She looked back at her phone. A video started playing, but the sound was off. She tapped the video to play it with the sound on.

"Which game is your organization playing?" the speaker asked, followed by intense music and several slides outlining possible games. Marie stared at the video as the screen had changed to "Game of Obfuscation." The speaker said: "Game of obfuscation, where you keep everyone guessing. For example, after promising to send out minutes after a meeting, instead, send out a loosely related report. If confronted, argue that this was the agreement the entire time. To win, you need to know the truth but also be able to bend it to your will."

Marie opened her mouth and audibly gasped. She felt that red-hot pool of anger bubbling up inside her stomach. This is the game that Mark is playing. This is why he didn't send me the link to the exit interviews. To keep me off balance. This is why I feel crazy around him.

On Monday morning, Marie thought about the game of obfuscation on her drive to work. The realization that Mark was intentionally creating confusion flipped everything on its head. Somehow, before this realization, she had been able to assume that he was just incompetent and, therefore, innocent.

Then she thought about her conversation with Anne. What hurt the most was that Anne had accused her of being the reason Paul was disengaged. Marie wanted them to form an effective HR management team. She wanted Paul to be her partner. After he stopped going to the HR breakfast, she gave up. If the seven people in HR can't work together, how is the company supposed to function as a unified whole? Suddenly, it struck her. What game was Anne playing? Anne was even more intent on speaking with Marie than Marie was on speaking to Anne. Why did Anne care about Zebra Apps at all? Anne left the company almost a year prior.

As Marie walked up the stairs to her office, she met Natalie walking down.

"Marie!" Natalie exclaimed. "I was just heading to your office. Mark told me about the good work you've been doing over the last week, and I'm excited to hear more about the culture program you're going to launch."

Marie was baffled. "The culture program ..." she repeated.

"Yes, to fix our retention problem," Natalie said.

Marie smiled but couldn't quite find a facial expression fitting for the situation. What had Mark promised Natalie?

"I'm just happy it's such an easy fix," Natalie said. "I was worried we might have to raise everyone's salaries."

Marie kept smiling.

"I can't wait to see your presentation on Wednesday," Natalie said. "You have my full support." Natalie turned around and walked back up the stairs.

Marie couldn't seem to move from her spot. She put her laptop bag down on the stairs and sat down. She thought, *Alright; apparently, I have a presentation to create about a culture program we are launching. And I am presenting that on Wednesday.* She could feel her stomach heating up and her jaw clenching. She grabbed her bag and headed toward Mark's office.

Mark wasn't in his office. As she headed back to her own office, she saw Mark walking down the hall. "Mark!" she shouted and picked up her pace, almost setting into a run.

He looked at her and smiled casually.

"We need to talk," she said.

"Sure, come on in," he said. "Don't you want to put your stuff in your office first?"

Marie noticed that she was still wearing her coat and scarf. "No, let's talk now," she said, heading straight for his office. She sat down in the chair across from Mark's desk. Mark leisurely walked in and sat down, stretching his legs out underneath his desk. "What did you promise Natalie?" Marie cut straight to the chase.

Mark looked at her, his lips quivering slightly. "I told her about the good work you've done researching why people are leaving," Mark said. "You know, like you and I spoke about in your office, that it's a culture thing."

"And what did you tell her we would do about it?" she asked.

Mark shifted in his seat. "Like we already discussed, you're going to do a presentation about the culture program we're going to make," he said.

Marie looked at him and couldn't believe she hadn't seen it before. He was bending reality to his will. "So, we're making a culture program," she mirrored.

Mark suddenly smiled, and his eyes lit up. "Not *we*, Marie—*you*," he said. "You're tasked with fixing our culture problem, remember?"

Marie felt the pool of lava pouring all the way down to her toes. He was going to make this hard for her. He wanted to see her fail, to get her off balance. She remembered the post on LinkedIn. She stood up from her chair and looked Mark straight in the eyes. His eyes shifted ever so slightly from side to side. Then she turned on her heel and went to her office.

Sudden Support

After taking off her coat and picking up a sheet of A3 paper from the copy room, Marie realized it was time for the coaching session with their new VP of sales, Jaque. By 9:10 a.m., Marie had already finished her coffee. There was still no sign of Jaque. She decided to wait another five minutes.

All new executives had to attend mandatory monthly coaching with Marie. This policy was Natalie's idea, but her support of it seemed to be subject to the influence of her leadership team. Especially Jaque. He had been their first sales executive. Before him, all sales were to existing clients or through referrals. After ASLO showed promise for scalability, the board decided that Zebra needed to professionalize. Jaque was recruited from ConvoSystems, where he was the VP of sales. He was not well-liked by Zebra's engineering teams—not even by Jenni, their CTO and head of engineering, who joined after Jaque.

Marie heard Jaque's voice speaking on the phone. It was 9:15 a.m.

"Let me just check if she's still here," he said, and she could hear his footsteps approaching the conference room. He peeped through the door, waved at Marie, and pointed to his phone. His black curls were as shiny as his dark gray suit. Marie nodded at him. "Jesus, she's still in there," she heard him say.

Marie felt her blood rushing to her face.

"I've got to go," Jaque said. "Last time I didn't show up, Natalie was pissed."

Marie didn't hear any footsteps approaching. Now, he was just standing there. *I wonder what game this guy is playing?* she thought. *The avoidance game,* she chuckled. He was trying to close his eyes and pretend she didn't exist. Marie got up from her chair and walked into the hallway. Jaque was scrolling on his phone and looked up at her in surprise.

"This is the last time you're late," Marie said, looking him straight in the eyes.

"I have better things to do than sit around talking about my feelings," he said.

"I don't care about your feelings," Marie said. "This is not about you. It's about creating a leadership team capable of running this company."

He huffed. "I was perfectly capable of running sales at ConvoSystems without spending time with HR," he said.

"Were you capable, Jaque?" Marie said and raised her eyebrows.

"What are you implying, Marie?" he said, taking a step toward her.

Marie took a deep breath. Finally, there was an opening to start the real conversation. "It doesn't matter how capable you are individually in the leadership team; it takes self-reflection and emotional maturity to be part of a team that pulls the organization in the same direction. We meet once a month, so I can help you develop those skills."

"Are you saying I'm emotionally immature?" he asked with a neutral face.

"Well, you've been hiding from me for the past five minutes," she said with a smile.

He smiled back. "OK," he said, heading to the conference room.

After spending an hour and a half with Jaque, Marie threw herself into her office chair. There was a tiny crack in Jaque's tough exterior. She knew how important developing the people in the leadership team was for the success of the company. But this was draining. She needed support. Natalie and Mark had already shown that they didn't intend to provide it. In fact, Mark seemed bent on undermining whatever success she had. She sent out a calendar invite to her team for the following day. Sending the invitation helped to lower her shoulders. She stretched her arms over her head, and her upper back cracked.

Eric, the most senior member of her team, knocked on her door. "Let's go get lunch," he said. Marie looked at her clock. It was 11 a.m.

Marie had forgotten how being part of the lunch crowd felt. As she filled her plate, she noticed the chef springing in and out of the line, piling food onto a plate. He saw Marie and suddenly stopped.

"Chef," Marie said.

"I was putting aside a plate for you," he said.

Marie looked down at her own plate. She had appreciated this gesture last week, but she couldn't quite read why the chef was doing her such a favor again. She looked up. The chef approached her.

"Let's see what you've picked out," he said, looking at her plate.

"Bread, lasagna, all three salads," he said. He showed her what he had been putting aside for her. Bread, lasagna, and all three salads.

"I'm glad you're finally having a proper lunch," he said. He leaned forward, almost whispering in her ear, "And my name is Joseph, not Chef." He smiled again and took his version of Marie's plate back to the kitchen with him.

As Marie was sitting down, Andrea sat down across from her. Willie sat next to Eric. Willie used to be a janitor but had retrained to be part of the hardware team that Simon used to run.

"Hey, Marie," Andrea said. Her voice sounded lighter now, and she was dressed in black pumps, black slacks, and a black turtleneck. Her shoulder-length hair was in a French braid. "It feels like I haven't seen you in forever," Andrea said. Then she looked into Marie's eyes. "It's really good to see you."

Marie smiled. "Eric made sure that I came to lunch today," Marie said, nudging Eric gently with her elbow.

"Good colleagues are golden," Andrea said. She leaned in across the table. "Speaking of colleagues," Andrea said in a hushed voice, "Anne called me on Saturday."

"Oh," Marie said, her mind suddenly racing back to her conversation with Anne. Her heart started pumping faster. Had she said too much? Anne hadn't known about Andrea's transition. Marie had been the one to tell her.

"Yeah, it was hilarious," Andrea continued. "Someone had obviously told Anne about my 'situation,' and she wanted to show her support."

"Hilarious?" Marie repeated, feeling the hairs rise on her arms.

"She wouldn't say my name or any pronoun," Andrea said. "You know, it was all, 'Hey you …', 'How are you doing …', 'Anything new …', that kind of stuff." Andrea laughed a bubbly laugh and shook her head. "I let her suffer for a couple minutes, then told her all about it," Andrea said.

Marie laughed a forced laugh. "How was that for you?" Marie asked.

"I was really happy that she called," Andrea said. "For everyone here, it's been easy to follow my transition, but I forget about all the people who left before anything happened on the outside." She gestured circles around her chest area.

"Yeah," Marie said, "I was thinking more about the business case situation—remember, the one about the spare capacity of the data center."

Andrea gave her a questioning look.

Now Marie was the one to lean in across the table. "When I found you in the bathroom …" she almost whispered.

"That was a tough week," Andrea said. "I'd just upped my dose of hormones and was adjusting."

Marie looked at her, confused. "You weren't upset about the business case?" Marie asked.

"I *was* upset about the business case," Andrea said firmly, "upset that we were making a business case for selling the spare capacity of the data center when we could have donated it to displaced children and teachers from Ukraine *and* broken even cost-wise from donations."

Marie felt her world turning upside down. In this story, Anne and Simon had somehow been the villains in her mind. Villains for putting Andrea in a tough situation during a difficult time. She was slowly realizing that Andrea wasn't a victim. And Anne and Simon weren't villains, meaning Marie was no longer the hero either.

"It was nice to speak to her," Andrea's voice broke through Marie's thoughts.

"I met with her last Friday," Marie said.

"Anne mentioned that you showed up early to your appointment," Andrea said. "Knowing Anne, that would throw her off. She likes to prepare."

"We were both half an hour early," Marie said.

"She can be intense, I know," Andrea said.

Marie nodded.

"Why did interest in the business case suddenly disappear, anyway?" Andrea asked.

"It didn't make it onto the leadership agenda," Marie said, having a hard time holding back a smile.

Andrea looked serious.

Willie got up to leave the canteen. "You know, we still have spare capacity in the data center," he said. "Those salespeople aren't filling orders as they promised."

"I wonder if the donors would still be willing to support rolling out ASLO to Ukrainian refugees," Andrea said, mostly to herself.

"I don't know how relevant that would be anymore," Marie said.

"The war is dragging on longer than anyone expected," Eric said.

"We still have spare capacity in the data center, and we've wasted our chance to contribute to a pressing need," Andrea said. She got up and picked up her tray. "Whatever happened to 'children's brains are not for commercial gain?'" Andrea said and walked away.

Eric and Marie were the only people remaining at their table. Marie looked down at her plate of untouched food. "This is why I started coming down later for lunch," Marie said. "I never get any eating done during lunchtime."

"We still have a couple of minutes," Eric said.

She dug into her salads. They sat in silence for a couple of minutes while Marie chewed. Suddenly, a thought struck her. "Where does it come from originally?" she asked Eric.

"Where does what come from?" he asked.

"Children's brains are not for commercial gain," she said.

"Jason always ended his presentations with that," he said.

"But where did Jason get it from?" she asked.

Eric thought for a couple of seconds. "I think it might have come from the mission statement that Natalie wrote when she founded the company," Eric said.

Marie raised her eyebrows.

"It's not on our website anymore, but I think it's still on the company drive," Eric said.

Marie put her knife and fork down on her plate and stood up. "Let's find out," she said.

The Original Mission

On the way up the stairs from the canteen with Eric, Marie spotted Jason walking down. It was his last week with Zebra. He looked at Marie and quickly looked down.

"Jason, you might know this. Marie and I were just talking about where the phrase you always used in your presentations—'Children's brains are not for commercial gain'—comes from?" Eric asked.

Jason looked up. "It was something Natalie said during my job interview," he said. "It was the reason I joined Zebra."

"So, it does come from Natalie," Marie said.

"Yeah, you can't really tell anymore," he said.

Eric put a hand on Jason's shoulder. Marie and Eric continued up the stairs to their floor. Eric pushed the door, intending to hold it open for Marie. Instead, the door bumped into something on the other side, only opening a sliver.

"Just a minute!" someone yelled on the other side of the door.

Eric shrugged.

"Clear!" the voice on the other side shouted.

Eric opened the door, and they both walked through. To the right of the stair door, next to Mark's office, workers were installing a fridge with a glass door.

"What in the ..." Marie said.

Mark came out of his office. "Nice, huh?" he said.

"What's this for?" Eric asked.

"It's a soda fridge," Mark said. "We'll install one on each floor."

Marie's eyes widened.

"Thanks to Marie's research, we now know that this is the key parameter that differentiates us from our competitors," Mark continued, "so we're closing the gap." Mark crossed his arms and smiled from ear to ear.

Eric and Marie exchanged glances.

"And Natalie approved this?" Marie asked.

"Of course," Mark said, waving his hand as if he was brushing Marie's question away.

"Mark, do you really believe that soda is going to make a difference?" Eric asked.

Marie looked at him, admiring his courage.

"At least we can say that we listened to what the employees wanted and did something about it," Mark said and went back to his office.

Eric shook his head.

Marie couldn't help but pace back and forth in her office. *Free soda,* she scoffed. *He isn't even trying to solve the problem.* She took a deep breath and shook her arms and torso as if trying to shake off Mark's stupidity. She noticed the A3 paper that she had picked up in the morning. "Just focus on what you can control," she said aloud and folded the sheet into thirds.

When she was a consultant, she had been thrown into a client assignment on a tight deadline without any explanation or context. This situation felt similar. Thinking through her options in a structured way used to help her. She started brainstorming on the sheet.

> *I am interested in getting to the bottom of the retention problem. Mark is interested in signaling that HR is doing something. I think that Natalie is also interested in solving the retention problem itself.*

She kept writing.

> *I want ASLO to succeed. It cannot reach its potential unless all departments in Zebra pull in the same direction.*

She looked up and thought, *Why aren't we pulling in the same direction?* She looked at her whiteboard. Her notes from last week were still there, with the word culture circled. *Perhaps some good could come out of a culture program,* she thought.

Jason knocked on the glass next to her door, and she waved him in.

"I looked through my email," he said, "and found the company presentation that Natalie showed me when I met her during my interviews."

"Oh," Marie said, not quite following.

"That's where it's from," he said. "Children's brains are not for commercial gain."

Marie's face lit up. "So, you have it?" she asked.

There it was. The onboarding presentation that Natalie used to do for all employees before she delegated it to Mark, who had since delegated it to Marie. The slide was simply headed "Our Core Beliefs" and followed by a single line: "Children's brains are not for commercial gain."

Marie felt a wave of hope wash over her. If Natalie was the originator of these words, she must believe in them.

"She sent it to me after my interview," he said. "This presentation is what convinced me to join."

Marie looked into his eyes, but Jason looked away.

"What else does it say?" Marie asked.

Jason scrolled through. There was a slide about the founding of Zebra by Natalie and her original cofounder, Richard; Natalie was an educator, and Richard was a technologist. It detailed how Natalie wanted to give teachers more time to interact with students and how Richard wanted to create game-like learning experiences. Richard was no longer with the company. He left before Marie joined.

There was a slide about what Zebra Apps did. There was also a slide showing the organization of Zebra Apps. Natalie was at the top, the board of directors in a box to the side. HR, finance, and facilities were on the left of the slide, and the developer teams were in two boxes categorized as "front-end" and "back-end." No managers were listed, just the individual developers.

"Remember when we all had to answer the phone when customers called us?" Jason said. "We complained so much that Natalie started hiring customer support."

Marie nodded. "I was the one to argue that developers' time was better spent developing," Marie said, "and that specialization was a natural part of commercial expansion."

"Maybe if we were still answering calls from clients, we would have maintained our organic growth," Jason said, "and wouldn't need to hire salespeople."

"Scaling is hard on all companies," Marie said.

"I didn't realize how good we had it," Jason said, changing slides.

There was the "Our Core Beliefs" slide again, this time detailing Zebra's values.

Marie sat up in her chair. "Wait a minute," she said.

There they were—Zebra Apps' values as Natalie and Richard had intended them: curiosity, collaboration, courage, commitment.

"That's it," Marie said. Jason looked at her. "Natalie has asked me to initiate a culture program," she explained. "I didn't realize we had already defined Zebra's values."

"I'll send you this presentation," he said. Without looking up, he continued, "It's weird to me that HR doesn't know the company's values." He looked up. "No offense."

Marie gave him a half-smile. "I completely agree," she said.

After Jason left her office, Marie considered how the values could have disappeared from their onboarding presentation. They weren't in the deck that Mark had shared with her. Had he been the one to remove them? She printed the deck. Walking back from the printer, she saw Joseph stocking the new fridge with soda from a trolley full of soda boxes.

"Is this your job now?" Marie asked.

Joseph looked at her and smiled.

"We must have someone else who can stock fridges," she said.

"The kitchen is short-staffed," Joseph said. "Of all my team members, I'm the most expendable."

"What?" Marie said. "You make the kitchen run."

"I'm not the one doing the cooking," he replied, "and right now, I'm not the one doing the dishes after lunch."

Marie suddenly had a realization. She was wrong to assume he was trying to be nice to her by setting her aside some lunch. Joseph was delivering a service to his customers. She was a customer. Now, he was protecting his team from stupidity by taking on this additional task himself. "Let me know if I can help expedite a hire for you," she said.

"You know, I will," he said. "This will be a full-time job."

Marie smiled to herself. Now Joseph is my customer.

She walked over to Eric and Sheila's desks. "Look what Jason found," Marie exclaimed proudly, putting the printed presentation in front of Eric.

"What is it?" Sheila asked curiously, standing up from her desk.

"The original onboarding deck that Natalie made," Marie said.

Eric started leafing through it.

"Look at slide four," Marie said.

"Natalie coined it," he said. "Children's brains are not for commercial gain."

"I thought Jason made that up," Sheila said.

"Now look at slide five," Marie said.

Eric turned the page.

"I present to you our core beliefs," Marie said triumphantly. "Aka the values of Zebra Apps. Well defined but long forgotten."

"We have values?" Sheila said, grabbing the page from Eric's hand and accidentally brushing her box braids on his face.

"It's a solid starting point for our culture program," Eric said.

Revisiting The Roots

The realization that Natalie was the source of the company's original cultural values had energized Marie and her team. Heading down to the conference room for a team meeting, Marie saw one of her team members, Jo, carrying some A2 sheets rolled up under her arm.

"Did you have posters made?" Marie asked.

"We may actually have a shot at changing the culture around here," Jo said. "I'm doing my part."

Walking into the conference room, they saw Eric and Sheila debating over a drawing on the whiteboard. Jo started taping her poster to the wall. Marie smiled. She was not alone on her mission.

As Jo and Sheila completed a draft plan for the culture program, Eric took Marie aside. "There must be a reason why these values dropped off the presentation. We're assuming they're still valid and that Natalie is behind them," Eric said.

"I think she's still behind them," she said, waving her hand as if to brush his statement away.

"You're assuming that Mark ditched them," Eric said.

"Well, yes," she said.

"Maybe, but Mark left our former employer because he found a better 'cultural fit,'" Eric said, making air quotes.

Marie remembered that Eric used to work for Mark at another technology company. She looked at him. "You think he was fond of the values?" she asked.

"That's what he told me when he left," he said. "Did you know he tried to persuade our old leadership team to consider establishing self-managed teams in our development organization? He put all his credibility on the line to run a pilot."

"I didn't know they had self-managed teams at Sailtech," Marie said.

"They don't," Eric laughed. "The pilot failed to take off, and Mark left."

"Oh," Marie said.

"I know that you and Mark haven't exactly seen eye to eye lately, but keep an open mind about him," Eric advised. "And probably run the plan by Natalie before you present it to the leadership team."

As Marie headed upstairs to her office, she thought about Mark. When she first started at Zebra Apps, she felt lucky she got to work for him. He used to speak at conferences and chaired a network about the future of work. She felt the lava ball rising in her stomach again. The last time she heard him present at a conference, he spoke about the four-day work week. It was so divorced from the reality of what she had experienced at Zebra Apps. Mark was always the last one to leave the office. He wouldn't leave before Natalie.

Whose Values Are They Anyway?

Marie glanced through the glass pane next to Natalie's office door and saw that Natalie's chair was empty. She looked around the floor. All the offices were empty. Marie spotted a fridge next to the stairway door, stocked with soda. She rolled her eyes and walked closer to it. Her eyes stopped to rest on a yellow Post-it note on the side of the fridge. Written in black Sharpie, the note said: "This is bullshit."

"Ha!" Marie exclaimed.

Celine popped her head out of her office, which was next to the fridge. Celine was Natalie's assistant. She had a Master's degree in marketing and strategy, but mostly spent her days managing Natalie's calendar.

"Are you the fridge vandal?" Celine asked. "Someone hung Post-its with insults on all the soda fridges," she explained.

"They were only installed yesterday," Marie replied.

"The notes were there this morning," Celine said.

Marie thought back to when she passed the fridge on her own floor this morning. "I didn't notice Post-its on the others," Marie said.

Celine shrugged. "The one in the canteen reads 'You suck,'" she said.

Marie smiled. Such an innocent rebellion but such a strong statement. Then she turned to Celine. "Do you know when Natalie is due back?" she asked.

"Let me take a look," Celine said, popping back to her desk. Marie followed her. "She's speaking at the Education Ministry today," Celine said.

"That explains why none of them are here," Marie said.

"Yes, the whole leadership team went together," Celine said, "except Mark."

Marie forced herself not to smile at that thought.

"They should be back this afternoon," Celine continued. "Natalie asked me to order dinner for her at the office." Celine looked up at Marie. "What do you think I should order," she asked, "the salmon or the steak?"

"I would go with the salmon," Marie said.

Marie walked past the fridge on her way to the staircase. The note was gone. She opened the door and caught a glimpse of Mark walking down the stairs, the Post-it glued to his index finger. Marie counted to sixty in her head before heading down.

Marie spent the late afternoon writing up a presentation explaining the two steps in the culture program that her team had defined that morning. She suggested taking the leadership team away for a half-day offsite to verify that the values were still a good fit for the company. Then, they would hold a town hall meeting to re-introduce the values to the rest of the company and have teams debate how the values should be translated into actions.

She looked at her watch—5:25 p.m. Natalie must be back by now. She took a deep breath and walked to Mark's office. Mark was still in, as expected, his chair turned toward his window. Marie rolled her eyes. *Like goddamn Don Draper*, she thought.

"Hey, Mark," she said.

He jumped in his seat and turned around without a word. His face was devoid of any mimicry. Marie felt no compassion toward his lack of facial expression.

"I'm ready to show Natalie the preliminary culture program," she said.

Mark got up from his chair and joined her. They walked in silence.

Natalie was standing in Celine's doorway. She smiled at Marie and Mark. "Here comes HR," she greeted them. "Celine already warned me that you were coming." She sat in her desk chair.

Marie almost bumped into Mark when sitting down—he usually sat in the chair right across from Natalie, but for some reason, he now chose to sit in the other chair. Mark smiled a faint smile.

"What do you have for me?" Natalie said.

"I want to show you the culture program deck before we take the whole leadership team through it," Marie said.

"It isn't due for another week," Natalie smiled. "Where do you get the time, Marie?"

Mark looked at Marie.

"My whole team contributed to this deck," Marie said. "We had a workshop this morning."

Suddenly, Mark sat straight up in his seat. "Do you mean you involved the entire department in creating a presentation?" he said loudly.

Marie looked at him and saw anger on his face. Somehow, it was preferable not to be able to read his emotions.

"Let's see it," Natalie interrupted.

Mark slumped back in his chair.

Marie took Natalie and Mark through the slides without stopping for comments or feedback. Natalie was taking notes. Mark was looking past the screen into the distance. After going through the town hall concept, Marie paused.

"Where did you get these?" Natalie said.

Marie shifted her gaze from the screen to Natalie. "The values?" Marie asked.

Natalie nodded.

"Jason showed me the onboarding deck you sent him when you interviewed him," Marie said.

Natalie sat back in her chair and clicked her pen. Suddenly, Marie felt uneasy. Would Jason get in trouble for sharing the company's values?

"I think building on the company's existing values is prudent," Mark said.

Marie looked at him, puzzled by the sudden support.

Natalie didn't even glance at him. She sat back up, looked at Marie, and said, "This is good work, Marie. I'm sure the entire leadership team will support this initiative."

"I'm glad to hear it," Marie said as she unplugged her laptop and got up to leave.

"Mark, can you stay a minute?" Natalie asked.

Mark had already gotten up to leave but sat back down in his unusual chair.

"Could you sit across from me?" Natalie gestured toward the chair that Marie just left.

Mark slowly got up and changed chairs.

Marie closed the door behind her and walked toward the staircase. She turned around and glanced through the window next to Natalie's door. Mark was gesturing with his arms as he spoke. *What is that about?* she thought. She walked across the hallway. The door to the staircase opened, and Celine came in with a takeout bag.

"It's the salmon," she said.

Marie was packing her bag in her office when Mark passed by her door in the hallway. She walked out of her office and followed him. "Are you OK?" she asked.

He looked up at her. "Today is not the best day," he said. He put his hand in his pocket and pulled out a handful of crinkled Post-its. He put them on the table in front of him and straightened out a pink one. "You suck," he read aloud. He unfolded an orange one: "To sweeten the suck," he read again. Then he read a yellow one: "This is bullshit." He looked at Marie. "They are right, you know."

Marie's jaw dropped.

"The soda fridges aren't going to stop people fleeing Zebra," he said. Then he turned around and looked out the window again. "I'm tired, Marie," he said.

She walked over to the window so she could see his face.

"Those values," he said. "Those are why I joined Zebra. I thought it would be different here."

Marie thought for a minute. "They were already defined when you joined," she stated.

"Natalie and Richard had a vision for how it should feel to be part of this company," he said.

"Did they define them together?" she asked.

"I think that they brought out the best in each other," he said, "but when Zebra got into cash flow problems, Natalie blamed his idealism."

"That's when the new investors came in," Marie suddenly understood.

"Yes, and Richard left the company," Mark said, "Natalie decided that he had been soft, and now it was her job to be hard."

Marie sat on the windowsill across from Mark. "How did they disappear from the intro deck?" she asked.

Mark smiled. "I took them out," he said. "There was too much dissonance between how we were as a company—or at least how we were becoming—and the values we had defined. I couldn't just stand there and lie to people's faces about what kind of company we are."

"But you're the head of HR," Marie said. "It's within your authority to change this."

"Maybe we still can," he said. "Marie, you'll need to win over Jaque. Natalie won't support you unless you get him on board."

"Because he is the right kind of hard?" Marie asked, half-joking.

"He's all about sales, and Natalie has sworn never to have a dry pipeline again," he said. Then he looked at her. "You know Todd from ConvoSystems, right?"

Marie nodded.

"See if you can get him to give you any tips on how to get on his good side," Mark said.

"What about Frank?" Marie said. "Should I be worried about our CFO?"

"Frank only cares about our quarterly numbers," Mark said.

As Marie walked down the stairs to her car, she looked at her clock again—7:15 p.m. Ally would be asleep by the time she got home. For the first time in months, she and Mark were on the same side—facing a problem together. Maybe Eric was right. Maybe she should postpone judgment of Mark. Her mind wandered to Jaque and Frank. She had little hope of getting Jaque's engagement. Frank O'Hara had been the CFO of Zebra from the beginning, so she had never coached him. She had only spoken to him during the annual budget rounds. She texted Todd from ConvoSystems and set the GPS for home.

New Alliances

Todd couldn't fit in a coffee appointment until the following Thursday. Marie waited for him in the coffee shop. She sat in the same chair at the same table as when she had met Anne. Frankly, she wasn't sure she needed this coffee meeting anymore. The previous night, she had presented the culture program to the entire leadership team. There had only been one question from the CTO, Jenni, on whether this initiative would take her developers away from their day jobs. Neither Jaque nor Frank had any questions or comments. It felt like a major win for her and the HR development team. The only concern she had was the look on Mark's face after the unanimous approval. He looked like he was suffering.

Todd approached Marie.

"Hey, Todd," she said as she hugged him. They ordered drinks and sat down. Todd was having tea.

"I'm trying to time my caffeine intake with my natural body clock," Todd said.

"Is this the focus of HR at your company?" Marie said.

Todd laughed. "No, it's just me," he said. "We're trying to take our culture program to the next level. We just contracted Anne to help us."

"Anne! Our Anne?" she said.

"She hasn't been 'your' Anne for almost a year now," Todd said.

"What does the next level even mean?" Marie asked.

"Over the past two years, we've come to a company-wide clarity about what it means to be at ConvoSystems—how we want it to feel to work for us, what that requires us to do, and how we deal with disagreements or behaviors that challenge how we aspire to be," Todd said. "Now we're ready to start re-organizing our organizational structure to fit our values."

Marie let it sink in. Two years to achieve clarity on values. An exercise she had planned would take two hours at a town hall.

"Anne is all about designing systems, so it makes sense you would bring her in at this stage," Marie said.

"Exactly," Todd said, smiling, "we were very pleased that she agreed to join us on this journey."

Marie felt like rolling her eyes. Journey was one of those bullshit words that always triggered her.

"We have another ex-Zebra joining us, too," Todd said, then paused to look around the room. "Do you want to know who?"

Marie nodded faintly.

"Richard!" he said, almost shouting as he raised his arms.

"What!" Marie leaned into the table, almost bumping her cup.

"The press release is coming out later today," he said, "so I'm just about not violating anything by telling you." He was smiling from ear to ear.

Marie was stunned. Richard joining ConvoSystems was a big scoop. After leaving Zebra Apps, he had mainly been doing interim management as CTO for edtech startups. Marie never imagined that he would take a job at a corporation the size of ConvoSystems. Then it hit her. Maybe that was what the heated exchange between Mark and Natalie was about the other day. Maybe one of them had gotten the news about Natalie's cofounder joining ConvoSystems.

"That is major," Marie finally said, "but didn't you have a CTO already?"

"Yes, we did," he said solemnly, "but he felt that ConvoSystems was no longer a company that he could imagine himself at."

"Why not, if I may ask?" she said.

"Our culture attracts great people like Richard now," Todd said, "but it's not for everybody."

Then Todd looked at her with a sparkle in his eye. "Some of them are leaving for Zebra," he said.

"We won't be leading on salaries anymore," she said.

Todd raised one eyebrow.

"We've installed soda fridges now," Marie said with a straight face.

Todd burst out laughing. Marie held a straight face for a couple of seconds but then started laughing until she couldn't breathe.

"Seriously, though," Marie said, still chuckling, "I wanted to talk to you about Jaque. Although, I'm not sure he will be as big of a problem for our culture program as I'd feared."

"You're embarking on a culture program?" Todd said.

"Yes, the leadership team just approved it last night," Marie said.

"Congratulations!" Todd said, reaching out to touch Marie's shoulder. "That must have taken some convincing."

"Honestly, no—they all agreed to it without any comments," Marie said.

"Uh-oh," Todd said, his eyes widening.

Marie frowned. "What do you mean?" she said.

Todd held his breath. Finally, exhaling, he said, "It means either they don't know what they're starting or they're not taking your suggestion seriously."

Marie's eyes widened.

"Jaque would never agree to start a culture program like the one we went through at ConvoSystems," he said. "He didn't like the idea of empowering the infield sales team that our culture program led to; he just wanted to tell them what to do."

Marie looked at him in disbelief.

"You know it's the whole reason he left ConvoSystems, right?" he said, looking at Marie. "Once people felt safe enough to speak up, no one wanted to work for him anymore."

Marie sat back in her chair. It had seemed too easy. "Is there an angle with Jaque?" she asked, trying to find some hope to cling to.

"He's motivated by status and power," he said, "but he probably wants these things because that's what his peer group appreciates."

"He is a middle-aged white man," she said, "so that's a probable assumption."

"But if he's separated from his peer group," Todd continued, "you may be able to speak to his humanity."

Walking to her car, Marie thought about Jaque. How could she separate him from his peer group at the leadership offsite? How could she get beyond the layers of status and ego to find his compassion?

Marie's phone pinged. There was a message from Eric, saying, "Have you seen the press release from ConvoSystems?"

Marie sighed. This would be a shock for everyone at Zebra Apps. Whether they had known Richard personally or not, he was a legend.

Separating The Peer Group

Marie pulled up at the hotel where the leadership team was meeting for their offsite. The hotel was surrounded by a forest and close to the beach. The receptionist showed Marie to the conference center. Marie had booked four conference rooms, making good on Todd's suggestion to separate the leaders from their peers.

In each room, she set up a poster she had made the night before. The poster said:

Our core beliefs:

- *Children's brains are not for commercial gain*
- *Curiosity*
- *Collaboration*

- *Courage*
- *Commitment*

She thought back to Jason and Simon's joint farewell party a few weeks before. The development team had hosted the party in the company parking lot. Simon had shared that he was joining ConvoSystems as a software engineer. He had told Marie that the people he worked with were more important to him than the work he would be doing—and there was no one he would rather work with than Anne and Richard. Simon told Marie that Richard's vision for the data center and his ability to predict technology trends were why he had originally joined Zebra. And they were why he would follow Richard to any other company. This was the first time Marie had heard that Richard used to be a game designer and had designed the data center to support an immersive game-like experience for learning.

Marie heard voices coming down the hallway.

"Hey, Marie," Sheila shouted.

Marie opened her arms to give her a hug. "Glad you found it," Marie said before hugging Eric and Jo.

Jo put down her box of Post-its and markers on one of the side tables.

"You can pick any room you like," Marie said.

"Alright!" Sheila said and went into the room on the far right.

They planned to divide the leadership group so that there was one executive in each room, along with one of their HR team acting as a facilitator. Mark would facilitate for Natalie. Marie had agreed to that partly because he was her boss and partly because she felt he was genuinely trying to shield her from Natalie's foul moods. Ever since the night Marie had presented the culture program to Natalie, it was like she and Mark had tuned into the same radio frequency.

Natalie came into the main conference room, speaking on her phone. She held a finger up to signal that she needed a moment and walked over to the floor-to-ceiling window as she kept speaking.

"No, you don't understand," Natalie said, "it is a big deal. We didn't have a competition clause. Even if we did, ConvoSystems is not technically a competitor." After a pause, she finally shouted, "Just find a loophole, damn it!"

Natalie put her phone down and looked out the window. She smiled as she turned around, wearing the smile like it was an accessory. "I might have to take a couple of calls during the session," she said.

Marie took a basket from the side table in the room. "That's why I brought this," Marie said. "Put your phone in here."

Natalie's eyes widened.

"It's three hours, Natalie," Marie said, waving the basket toward her. "You can catch up on calls later."

Natalie tightened her lips and narrowed her eyes but put the phone in the basket. "Is there coffee in this place?" Natalie said, and she walked out of the room, no longer smiling.

Marie could hear Natalie greet Frank in the hallway. "Quick, hide your phone," Natalie roared.

Frank walked into the conference room. "Where do you want this?" he asked, holding his phone in his hand. Marie gestured at the basket.

Soon, Mark and Jenni arrived, too. It was almost 9 a.m., but there was no sign of Jaque.

"I would call him, you know," Natalie said with a half-smile, "but I literally can't."

The others snickered. Jaque walked in, biting into a croissant. He sat down quietly.

"Nice of you to show up," Natalie said.

"What—I'm on time," Jaque said, croissant crumbs falling from his mouth.

Marie walked over to him with the basket.

"Is it Christmas already?" he remarked.

"No, it's for you to put your phone in," Marie said.

"No," Jaque said.

"Surely a man of your stature can live without checking TikTok for three hours," Marie said.

The others laughed. Jaque put his phone in the basket.

Marie started by introducing the rediscovered values, explaining how Natalie and Richard had founded the company upon them. Natalie was quiet for most of the introduction. Marie was about to introduce their individual breakout sessions when Jenni interjected.

"If these are Zebra's values, why was I not introduced to them when I joined?" Jenni asked, looking at Mark.

Mark looked down at the table. Natalie looked at Marie.

"Sometimes focus in a company has its ebbs and flows," Marie said. "After Zebra experienced financial issues, we shifted our focus to making commercial progress."

Natalie smiled a barely distinguishable smile.

Jenni looked straight at Natalie. "Is this HR bullshit, or are you actually behind this?" she asked.

Natalie laughed nervously. "You all approved the culture program when Marie presented it to us in April," Natalie said.

"Don't try that on me, Natalie. I'm not the Education Ministry," Jenni scoffed.

"Are these the founding values or not?" Jaque chimed in.

Natalie stood up and walked to the end of the table. "You may remember that I used to be a teacher," Natalie said.

"Glad you're not teaching my kids," Jaque shouted.

Natalie raised an eyebrow. "It wasn't the teaching I became fed up with," Natalie continued, "it was how disempowering it felt to be a teacher in our school system."

Jaque sat up straight.

"When I met Richard, we wanted to create something that felt different. A company that made teaching about how children learn. Something that dignified teachers. We wanted to explore what that could look like—whether it was supported by technology or not. We even considered opening a school in the beginning." Natalie stopped and looked down at the floor. "We also tried working with some of the existing edtech providers at the time. But they weren't bold enough—they only wanted to support classroom-based teaching as it is, not attempt to re-invent it."

Natalie paused.

"When our initial products didn't pan out, we disagreed on how to handle it. Richard wanted to bet even more on gaming-like teaching experiences that required further investment. I wanted to find customers for the products we had already developed. So, Richard decided to take his commitment to Zebra Apps—and to me—and toss it in the bin." Natalie sat down and crossed her arms.

No one spoke.

Marie broke the silence. "There is history behind these values," she said, "and today we're going to try them on for size and see if they still align with the kind of organization we want to be."

She went on to explain the facilitated exercises.

Marie followed Jaque into the conference room furthest on the left. He sat down in the chair next to the poster on the whiteboard. "I'm starting to feel TikTok withdrawal setting in," he joked.

Marie smiled.

He looked at the poster. "What am I supposed to do again?"

Marie gave him a marker. "Let's start with brainstorming the meaning of each value," she said.

Marie was surprised to find Jaque engaged—even thoughtful. For "Courage," he elaborated on how his secret sauce for selling was to counter what the clients said they wanted with what they needed. "It's like you," he said, turning toward Marie, "when you call me out for being an asshole for dragging my feet in our coaching sessions or refusing to give my phone up."

Marie smiled and lifted her eyebrows.

"Commitment," he said and paused. "We don't see a lot of that at Zebra these days," he said. "People are quitting left and right, jumping off to competitors or God knows where."

"Why is that a lack of commitment?" she asked.

"It's a lack of commitment to Zebra," he said, raising his voice.

"But what is Zebra committed to?" she asked.

He turned a chair around and sat down facing the board. "To reaching our quarterly sales numbers," he said slowly.

Marie nodded.

"Was it different before?" he asked. "When this Richard guy was still here?"

"He wasn't here when I joined," Marie said, "but it was different back then."

He looked at her. "You know ..." he started, before pausing. "I've lived through another culture transformation. At ConvoSystems."

Marie nodded.

"It was all about employee empowerment and delegating responsibility downward to stay innovative," he said, gesturing an upward curve with his hand. "I was new to the sales director role back then," he continued, "and suddenly, no one was paying any attention to what I wanted to do."

Marie looked into his eyes.

"I had finally reached that stage where I got to be the one to decide and had to give that power away," he said. He shrugged his shoulders. "Of course, if I had the power to decide how I wanted to do my sales when I was a rep, I might never have climbed the ladder in the first place. Might have taken up golf!" He laughed.

Marie smiled. "Which of these values resonates most with you?" she asked.

"Collaboration," he said.

Marie raised her eyebrows.

"Are you surprised?" he asked.

"A little bit," she admitted.

"What I was trying to do at ConvoSystems was to get sales and marketing to work more closely together—ideally as one team," he said. "That, and working with customers, are the best ways to sell."

"Have you tried making it work here?" she asked. "Both sales and marketing are under your organization."

"You know I haven't," he said. "I guess I got my hands burned the last time I tried." Then he pointed to the poster. "Courage is what I have least of," he said.

After the break, Marie was calling everyone back to join in the main room when she saw Sheila. Her eyes were red, and she was wiping her nose with a Kleenex. Marie walked over to her. "Are you OK?" she asked.

Sheila shook her head. Marie ushered her into the closest meeting room.

"Are you sick?" Marie asked.

Sheila shook her head again. "He wouldn't say anything," she said.

"Who?" Marie asked.

"Frank," Sheila said. "The more he stayed silent, the more I spoke, and the angrier he looked."

"Where is he now?" Marie asked.

"He yelled at me and left the room," Sheila said.

"What did he yell?" Marie asked.

"Something like 'Now Natalie has really lost it,'" Sheila said, looking around the room.

"OK, go get some water to drink, then find Eric. I'll go look for Frank," Marie said.

Sheila nodded.

Marie went to the coffee room—no Frank. She went to reception and asked if they had seen an older man in a gray suit. They said that he had walked out to the parking lot. Marie went out there to look for his car. Realizing she didn't know what it looked like, she went back inside. She counted the phones in the basket. All five phones were still there.

"Are we starting now?" Jenni asked, startling Marie out of her thoughts.

"Yes, let me just get the others," Marie said.

At that moment, she saw Frank walking toward the hotel from the direction of the sea. Marie sighed with relief. He came back in, crossed his arms, and sat down in silence. Marie called Jaque, Natalie, and Mark back. For the remaining hour, they individually took turns sharing their definitions of a value and how it currently manifested in the organization.

Marie looked around the room. "Based on what you just shared," she said, "we do see these values at play in our organization."

Everyone nodded except Frank.

Natalie walked up to the front of the room. "Are we keeping these values or what?" she exclaimed.

Jaque, Jenni, and Mark clapped. Frank was motionless. As soon as Marie adjourned the meeting, Frank grabbed his phone from the basket and quickly walked out the door.

Natalie fished out her phone. It was ringing. "Hello," she said, "yes, thank you for looking into it." She walked toward the window again. "You know, on second thought, I don't want to pursue litigation." She sighed, and her shoulders fell. "Let him commit to ConvoSystems."

Operating System

The email came on Friday morning. Marie was on her way up the stairs for breakfast with her team as usual, cinnamon buns greasing the paper bag in her hand. She was about to check which meeting room they had set for breakfast when the email from Mark stopped her in her tracks.

> From: Mark Lawson
> To: Zebra Apps_All
> Subject: **Frank O'Hara is retiring**
>
> Effective immediately, Frank will be stepping down from his role as CFO.

> Frank was originally hired by the founders to help with the bookkeeping, but over time, he grew in his role to become our CFO.
>
> Frank will be enjoying time with his grandchildren and taking up golfing. We thank Frank for many years of loyal service to the company.
>
> The search for a new CFO has already begun.
>
> Kind regards,
> Mark

Marie let go of the bag of cinnamon buns. It fell all the way down to the basement. *Shoot,* Marie thought and walked down. The basement floor was full of stacked office furniture and server casings. She couldn't see her bag anywhere. Leaving the cinnamon buns was not a good option, but she didn't feel like rummaging through all the junk in the basement to look for the probably crushed buns. She decided to run to the coffee shop on the corner to get fresh ones.

There was a line at the coffee shop. As she tried to eye the counter to see how many cinnamon buns were left, she saw Simon, former manager of their data center, in line in front of her.

"Hey," Marie shouted.

He turned around. "Marie," he exclaimed and leaned over to hug her.

Ahead of Simon in the queue, Marie saw Anne.

"Hey, Marie," Anne said and extended her hand for a handshake.

"What are you two doing out together on a Friday morning?" Marie said.

"We're colleagues now," Anne said. "What about you?"

"I dropped my bag of buns down the stairwell," Marie said, grimacing.

"Down into the heap of junk?" Simon laughed.

"Yeah, you're never going to see those again," Anne laughed.

"How did the leadership offsite go?" Simon asked.

Marie looked at him. "If you'd asked me yesterday, I would've said that it was a roaring success," Marie said, "but I just got an email that Frank is retiring."

"Retiring or 'retiring'?" Simon asked, doing air quotes.

"What can I get for you?" the barista asked.

Anne ordered for her and Simon.

"I don't know," Marie said, "but it was very sudden."

"What happened during the offsite?" Anne asked, turning around.

"He shut down, really," Marie said. "Sheila was crying after facilitating with him."

"You put Sheila in the same room as Frank?" Anne asked, eyebrows raised.

Marie ordered five cinnamon buns to go and was handed a brown bag.

"Sheila is pure creative energy," Anne said. "Frank is all about the detail. They're like polar opposites that cancel out each other's energy."

"You're saying he left because I put him in a room with Sheila for an hour and a half?" Marie asked.

"Frank was hanging by a thread for a long time," Simon said. "Every time I went into his office, he would be shaking his legs and fidgeting."

"You went into his office?" Marie asked.

"Yes, he was actually a fun guy," Simon said.

"That you have to explain," Anne said. "Decent, hard-working, detail-oriented, yes—but fun?"

Simon smiled. "He was guy stuff fun," he said. "He loved Tintin and sailing—and he was a big supporter of any hardware I needed for the data center."

"Don't you miss your data center?" Marie asked.

"The data center is just servers," he said. "I don't miss being angry and feeling like I'm overlooked."

Marie was quiet for a minute.

"This is just the beginning, you know," Anne said.

"What do you mean?" Marie asked.

"When you start rocking the boat like you are, people will get angry," Anne said. "You can't stop until you've transformed the whole system."

"You and your systems," Marie said.

"An organization has an operating system," Anne went on. "Its operating system is its culture and ways of working. You've started scratching a corner of that in an organization with a lot of pent-up anger. Emotions are about to run high."

Sugar

It was Monday. Eric had managed to get Sheila, Jo, and Marie to come to the canteen at the same time. He had cornered Marie after her meeting with a potential external recruiter about hiring staff for the kitchen.

While circling the buffet table, Marie caught a glimpse of Joseph speaking to one of the kitchen staff. She walked over to him. He looked over at her and smiled.

"Just a sec, Marie," he said. He put a hand on the shoulder of the man he was speaking to and said, "We'll figure this out." The man nodded and headed back to the kitchen.

"Is he alright?" she asked.

"It's a great mystery, Marie," he said, throwing his hands up in the air.

Marie's eyes widened.

"All the sugar packets are gone," Joseph said. "Every one of them."

"What?" Marie said with a chuckle.

"Look at the tables," Joseph said, gesturing around the hall. "No sugar packets."

"The salt and pepper bags are still there, but the sugar is gone," Joseph continued.

"Did we start putting more sugar on our food?" Marie offered.

"You don't understand," Joseph said. "The sugar packets are also gone from the pantry."

"You're telling me that all the sugar packets—the ones from the tables and the ones from the pantry—are missing?"

"It's a mystery," Joseph said.

They both stood in silence for a few seconds. Marie noticed that her team had sat down. "I spoke to the recruiter today," she said.

Joseph looked at her.

"She seemed like a good bet to help us recruit the missing headcount for the kitchen," she said.

"That's good news, Marie," Joseph said.

"We can't have you stocking the soda fridges," Marie said.

"No, we need me solving sugar mysteries," Joseph said with a smile.

"There must be a logical explanation for this," Marie said.

Marie put her plate down at the table where her team was sitting. She noticed Joseph walking around the room, looking up at the security cameras. Jo and Eric were talking about the upcoming town hall. Sheila was looking down at her bowl. Marie tried to make eye contact.

"How's the pasta?" Marie asked.

Sheila looked up and gave her a half-smile.

Marie looked at her. This was hard to watch. Sheila was always the life and soul of any conversation. This was a gloom Marie had never seen before. She had to fight the urge to get up and give her a hug.

"It's not your fault, you know," Marie said.

Sheila looked at her.

"Frank left because he didn't want to be at Zebra anymore," Marie said, "not because of the leadership offsite."

Sheila put her fork down on top of her pasta. "You weren't in there with me," Sheila said. "It was bad." Sheila's eyes started to turn red. She shook her head. "I just couldn't stop myself," she said. "I knew that I needed to give him space, but I just went on talking." Sheila covered her eyes with her hands. "This is a nightmare," she mumbled.

Marie felt as if she had been struck on the back of the head. How could she have missed that Sheila felt so bad after the offsite? It had been five days. She met Eric's gaze. He nodded slightly at her. Suddenly, she understood why he was so keen on getting them all together for lunch.

"You fucked up," Jo said.

Sheila emerged from behind her hands and looked at Jo.

"It's no big deal, really," Jo continued. She leaned into the table. "Look, if you were making toothpaste caps, a fuckup would be using the wrong mold for the cap," Jo said, "but your line of work is coaching people, so when you make a mistake, you don't just get a weirdly shaped toothpaste cap—someone's feelings get hurt, and they resign."

Marie was about to interject. She wanted to say that Sheila didn't make a mistake—that none of this was her fault—but Jo carried on.

"At my former company, we used to keep a failure museum," Jo said. "Every time one of us had a disastrous training session with a client, we would exhibit it on a big pinboard in the canteen. We would drink failure mead from ugly clay mugs that one of our receptionists made in her spare time and talk it through."

Sheila suddenly lit up. "That's a great idea," she said.

Marie raised her eyebrows and looked at Sheila.

"That's like a standard operating procedure for dealing with failure," Eric said. "I'm in!"

"Let's do it this afternoon," Jo said. "We can start our own museum in Marie's office."

Now Marie felt like hugging Jo. "You can have my wall," she said, smiling.

"Sheila shouldn't be the only one to share a mistake," Eric said. "Let's all bring one."

Marie looked at Eric. Somehow, he always knew what to say.

"I'll bring a mistake to share," Marie said.

"But what do you share about your mistake?" Sheila asked.

"We used to follow four steps," Jo said. "First, you describe the mistake—what happened, where, when, who was there. Then, we categorize if it was a lapse in judgment or a bad outcome—I mean if it was something you could actually avoid or something outside your control. Then, we reflect on what needs to be different about the circumstances or your own behavior for it not to happen again. Lastly, we celebrate it. We would clink our clay mugs, raise our right hands, and shout 'To hell with it.'"

Eric raised an eyebrow.

"Now, at my old job, several of us were into Renaissance fairs; you could do something else," Jo explained, reacting to Eric's face. "The important thing is that you come together to acknowledge that a mistake was made—but that doesn't mean that the person who made it is excluded from the team."

"I love it," Sheila said. "Let's do it!"

"I'll bring mead," Eric smiled.

Mead And Balls

It was 3:10 p.m., and Marie was putting together the program for the quarterly town hall. This time, the town hall would be extended to two hours to make time to announce the rediscovered values. A knock on her door made her look up. Mark was leaning against the doorframe while resting a hand on the top of her door.

"That recruiter you spoke to today," Mark said, "any good?"

"They seem to have a lot of experience with hospitality staff," Marie said. "I would like to try them for Joseph's open positions."

"Good," Mark said, looking briefly into the hallway, then coming in and closing the door behind him. He sat down in the armchair. "We need to find a recruiter for the CFO position," he said.

"OK," said Marie, "I don't think this particular recruiter would be a good choice for that."

"No," Mark said, "I mean, in general."

Marie looked at him. She could feel that familiar warmth in her gut. Her jaw tensed.

"Would you like me to make some suggestions?" Marie asked.

"No," he said and rubbed his face with his hands. "I need someone to brainstorm with to figure out how we hire a better fit than Frank," he said.

The warmth from Marie's stomach rose to her cheeks. "Oh," she said, "I would be happy to brainstorm with you."

"Do you have time now?" he asked.

"Actually, the team is doing a failure celebration in about five minutes," she said. "We're going to use this wall as a failure museum." Marie gestured to the wall next to her whiteboard.

Mark smiled. "We did that with my old team at Sailtech once," he said. "I think Eric was there for that."

"It was Jo's idea," Marie said, "but Eric promised to bring the mead."

Mark raised his eyebrows.

"Apparently, that's a requirement," Marie said.

"Will there be any sacrifices—human or otherwise?" Mark said, tilting his head.

Marie laughed. "We may need an unsuspecting VP to appease the gods of failure," she said.

"Uh-oh," Mark said, looking around as if trying to avoid capture.

Marie looked at him and felt warm inside. Not in her gut, but in her chest. "Would you like to join our pagan ritual?" Marie said. "I mean without being sacrificed."

Mark smiled. "I think it's important to keep these rituals small," he said. "You need to have trust for people to really open up about their mistakes."

Marie nodded.

"But maybe I'll steal the idea for my team," he said, "and have a failure museum session of my own with you and Paul."

"Uh," Marie said, "lots of skeletons rattling in our closets."

"Maybe it's time we dusted them off," he said.

Marie took a deep breath.

"Let's brainstorm the CFO position tomorrow, then," Mark said and got up to leave. He looked back, "I appreciate the invitation, though."

As soon as Mark left, Eric entered Marie's office with a bottle of mead in hand.

"Where did you get this?" Marie asked. "And on such short notice?"

"Willie brews his own mead," Eric said. "He has a stash in his locker."

Eric looked more intently at Marie. "Don't you read the intranet posts?" he said. "Willie has been advertising this batch since February."

"Not much demand if he still hasn't sold the batch after four months," Marie said.

"He was pretty excited to have a customer," Eric said.

"Did he have any cups to go with it by any chance?" Marie said.

"Clayware isn't part of his product selection," Eric replied. "Let's just get some mugs from the kitchen."

While Eric was getting mugs, Jo came in. She nodded at Marie and started attaching a large piece of recycled brown cardboard to the wall.

"Where did you get that?" Marie asked, wincing at the sight of the slightly stained sheet.

"From the bottom of the stairwell," Jo said. "There is lots of great stuff down there."

Marie thought about the bag of cinnamon buns she had dropped into that heap of stuff at the bottom of the stairwell.

"You actually go there to find materials?" Marie asked.

"Yeah," Jo said, "why would we use new stationery when there is lots of perfectly good stuff down there?"

Marie bit her lip.

"Today, it really smells like cinnamon down there," said Jo, shrugging her shoulders.

She took a whiteboard marker and wrote the procedure for dealing with mistakes on the whiteboard. Finally, they were all gathered in Marie's office. Eric poured everyone mead.

"Who wants to share the first failure?" Jo asked.

"I'll go first," Marie said. "This is embarrassing, really."

"It always is," Jo said.

"You know our chef," Marie started. "I just recently learned his name."

"Joseph," Eric said.

"Until recently, I always called him 'Chef,'" Marie continued, "and he had to correct me himself."

"Why is this a mistake, Marie?" Jo asked.

"It was a lapse in judgment on my part," Marie said. "I hadn't considered him a colleague on an equal footing with—say—finance. Because he was a service provider, he somehow wasn't entitled to the same courtesy I extend to my other colleagues."

"That sounds like a bias," Sheila said.

"I agree," Marie said, "and I'm embarrassed by it, especially since I've observed how competent a leader he is. I could learn a lot from how he shows up for his team."

"What needs to be different so this mistake doesn't happen again?" Jo asked, nudging Marie to continue her analysis.

"I need to change my mindset," Marie said, "and categorize everyone working at Zebra as colleagues—and do my best to learn people's names."

"You can't know everybody's name," Eric interjected.

Marie thought for a moment.

"You're right, especially as we grow," Marie said, "so maybe it's more about noticing when I start describing someone by their function rather than their name—like 'the garbage collector' or 'the barista'—and take that as a sign that I need to ask the person's name."

"But, guys," Sheila said, "why is it important to know people's names in the first place? There are lots of people in my life whose names I don't know. My hairdresser, my nail lady, my dry cleaner."

"For me, it's about how I perceive people whose names I don't know," Marie said. "Somehow, they become more abstract, and I don't take their issues as seriously as those of the people I perceive as being part of my communities."

"My hairdresser was at my birthday party last month," Sheila said.

"What did you call her when you invited her to your birthday?" Jo asked.

"I just wrote 'HEY' in all caps in Messenger and said that she *must* come to my party," Sheila said.

Jo laughed, and Eric couldn't restrain himself either.

"Do you want to know her name?" Marie asked.

"I know she has dance moves," Sheila said. "I'll figure out her name eventually."

"I don't think my learning applies to you, Sheila," Marie said.

"How do you want us to celebrate your mistake?" Jo asked.

Marie was grateful that Jo was pushing the process forward.

"You can pick if we toast, dance, high-five, shout ..." Jo said. "Anything that we can do as a group in high spirits."

"Then I want to clink our mead mugs and shout huzzah," Marie said.

They all brought their mugs together and shouted, "Huzzah!"

"I was sure you were going to share the mystery of where the cinnamon buns disappeared to last week since you had to get new ones," Eric said.

Marie felt her cheeks heating up. She looked at the door. "I dropped them down the stairwell," she said.

"No way," Jo said, "that's why it smells like cinnamon down there!"

"Did you just leave them down there?" Sheila exclaimed.

Marie looked at her shoes. "Yes," she said.

"Noooooo!" chorused the team.

"I did go down there to look for them," she said, "but there were no signs of the bag. I would've had to start moving server casings around to find them."

"Marie! Rats are going to find that bag!" Jo gasped.

"I don't think we have any rats in the building," Marie said.

"We will have rats if we keep food lying around in the basement," Eric said.

Marie looked around at her team. She was not getting out of this. "Ugh, OK. I'll go look for the bag of buns after we're done here," she said.

"Huzzah!" Sheila screamed and clinked Jo's mug.

Jo took two Post-its and drew a rat on one of them and a nametag on the other. She gave them to Marie.

"All yours to put up in the museum of failure," Jo said.

"Do the buns really count as a mistake?" Marie pleaded.

"That was poor judgment alright," Eric chuckled.

Marie smiled back at him. It stung to admit that it was bad form to just leave the bag of buns there. But, somehow, having her whole team correct her felt good. She felt embraced. She put the two Post-its up on the cardboard sheet on the wall.

"Who's next?" Jo asked.

The failure museum soon featured a Post-it with a drawing of a calendar and a person pointing to a blackboard to symbolize mistakes shared by Eric and Jo.

"I think everyone has figured out what I'm going to share," Sheila said.

"It's completely up to you, Sheila," Jo said.

"No, I do want to talk about it," Sheila said, "and it did help to see how everyone's jobs are a bit of a mess."

Muttered laughter spread through the room.

"Start by describing it," Jo said.

"Alright," Sheila said, her voice breaking and eyes welling up. "I was waiting in the breakout room, not knowing who would walk in. When Frank came in, I was relieved at first because Jaque is so much more difficult to deal with." She took a deep breath. "Frank was very much to the point and wanted to get started with the exercise right away. He cut me off when I asked him how he found the breakfast and the surroundings."

"How did that make you feel?" Jo asked.

"It made me feel … wrong, I guess, like I had made a mistake," Sheila said. She thought for a moment.

"I was trying to make him feel at ease, or so I thought. Maybe I was trying to make myself feel at ease. Anyway, we started the exercise, and he was very brief on all points. It felt like he was trying to get through the whole thing as quickly as possible, and I started to doubt whether we were doing it right. I looked at my watch, and it seemed like we would be done at least forty-five minutes before we were supposed to. I started asking additional questions and telling him stories about other workshops I've done."

"Were his responses superficial?" Jo asked.

"No ... he was pretty much to the point," Sheila said, then paused. "I see now," she continued, "that he was being efficient, and maybe he thought he could get some work done or something if we finished early."

"How did you feel when he was being brief?" Jo asked.

"I felt like he was dismissing me," Sheila said.

"That's a lot of existential emotion to bring to a workshop," Jo said.

A tear ran down Sheila's cheek.

Marie looked at Jo. She felt like she was being harsh, but at the same time, she respected Jo's straightforward approach to the situation.

"What could have been different to avoid this situation?" Jo continued.

"It would have been easier if I'd known who was going to come in," Sheila said, "because then I could prepare and find an approach that fits the situation."

Marie suddenly felt like the room turned upside down. "Of course," she exclaimed, "we could totally have planned that upfront."

"I spent so much time worrying that I would have to deal with Jaque that I didn't consider what I would do if I had to work with Frank," Sheila said.

"That's a really good point, Sheila," Eric said. "We will plan that out next time."

"What happened right before he stormed out?" Jo asked.

"He started to fidget with his hands, and then his legs were jumping in his seat," Sheila said. "Then he stopped paying attention and got this blank expression on his face."

"What did you do?" Jo asked.

"I started talking louder and faster," Sheila said and hid her face in the palms of her hands. "Then he got up, tore open the door, and walked out," Sheila said. "He must have felt overwhelmed and trapped—to walk out like that."

"How would you categorize this mistake?" Jo asked.

"I think it's a bad outcome, but probably also bad preparation on my part," Sheila said, "and bad emotional management from me."

"What do you mean by that?" Jo asked.

"I think that I could have focused more on the task at hand and on Frank rather than being caught up in my own insecurities," Sheila said.

"Why were you so insecure in this situation?" Marie asked.

"This was my first time facilitating for the senior management team," Sheila said, looking at Marie.

"I hadn't thought of it that way," Marie said. "You're such a strong facilitator and coach that the thought of it being a big deal for you didn't even cross my mind."

Sheila looked at the floor.

"That's a lapse in judgment on my side," Marie said.

"I could have told you how I was feeling," Sheila said, "but it just seemed stupid and like I need to grow a pair."

"Now, that is an important lesson," Eric said. "Anytime you dismiss yourself by thinking that you need to grow a pair is a signal to talk to someone about how you're feeling."

Sheila nodded, and a tear dropped down her other cheek. Eric walked over to her and gave her a big hug. She sobbed into his shoulder, and he hugged her for a minute. Finally, Sheila emerged from his embrace, red-eyed but smiling.

Jo drew on a Post-it. She turned it around so everyone could see, and the whole team burst out laughing. The drawing was of a pair of balls.

Sheila added it to the museum wall.

"This makes me want to revisit our planning for the town hall," Marie said, "and go into a bit more detail about who does what and when."

"That would be great," Sheila said. "I am a bit nervous about it."

"I'll look for a time slot for us," Eric said, "preferably tomorrow."

"Before we move on," Jo said. "Sheila, how would you like us to celebrate you?"

"I want us to clink our mugs and shout 'to hell with it,'" Sheila said, her eyes sparkling.

They brought together their mugs, lifted them over their heads, and shouted, "To hell with it!"

Sheila clapped and smiled. Marie looked at her and felt her shoulders dropping. She also looked over at Jo and wondered how she could have missed what a hardcore facilitator she was. Sheila was always her go-to because she was so well-liked. Jo had struck her as a bit awkward and confrontational, but by being so calm and to the point, she had guided them through difficult conversations—without worrying about whether people would like her or not.

You Have Sugar On Your Hands

The next morning, Marie left for work while Thomas was still making Ally breakfast. She wanted absolute privacy for the first thing on her agenda—fishing out the cinnamon buns from the basement.

Her heart sank as she walked all the way down the stairs to the bottom of the stairwell. She really didn't want to look through the heap of junk. The only thing keeping her committed was how her team had reacted to her carelessness.

She paused on the last step. There was stuff layered right in front of the stairs. She walked back up a step to get a better overview. Thomas had discreetly pushed a flashlight into her hands as she kissed him goodbye that morning. He was also the one to suggest that she wear sneakers to climb around in the basement. She scanned the room with the beam of the flashlight. Nothing moved. There were no rats—not yet, at least. She sighed. She would have to step into the mess.

She stepped over an office chair lying on its side. Then she scraped past a metal box and some plastic tubes. She looked up the stairwell. There was still a way to go before she was directly under the likely path of the cinnamon bun bag, based on where she had been standing on the stairwell when she dropped it. She looked around for a path through. There was a stack of cardboard boxes next to her. She leaned on one of the boxes as she crawled onto the stack. Suddenly, her foot went through the box, and she let out an "Ah!" sound as her foot landed in something that felt like sand. She pulled it out, but her sneaker came off and fell into the box. Standing on one foot, she opened the box and retrieved her sneaker. As she put it back on, she looked in the box.

That looks like sugar, she thought.

She opened the top box in the stack. Also sugar.

"What are you doing down here?" she heard from behind.

The sudden comment made her jump backward. She tripped and landed on some plastic tubes.

"Ugh," she grunted.

"Are you OK?" the voice said.

She felt someone hold her under her armpits and pull her up. She came to a standing position and turned around. It was Willie, the once-janitor who retrained to be part of the hardware team.

"What are you doing?" Willie asked.

"I dropped a bag of cinnamon buns down here last week," she said, "and I was trying to find it so we don't get rats."

"I was wondering where that bag had come from," he said, "but I found it last night and threw it away."

"You've already found it?" Marie said.

"Yeah, it smelled pretty intensely down here," he said.

"Not my finest moment," Marie said.

"Now, get out of here," he said, pointing up the stairs.

Marie made her way over the tilted office chair and hurried up the stairs.

She was mortified that someone else had fixed her mistake. Suddenly, she came to a stop. *Wait a minute,* she thought. *Did he say he found the bag of buns last night? What was Willie doing in the basement on a Monday evening?* She looked down at her shoe covered in sugar. *And why were there boxes of sugar down there when sugar was going missing from the canteen?*

Marie was brushing the sugar off her sneaker into the bathroom sink when Jo walked in.

"I stepped into a box of sugar at the bottom of the stairwell," Marie explained.

Jo raised her eyebrows and chuckled. "You went back to find the cinnamon buns?" she asked.

"Yeah, but it turns out that Willie had already found them and thrown them out," Marie said.

"You have some white streaks across the back of your blazer," Jo said.

Marie put her shoe down on the floor and took the blazer off to inspect the back.

"Must be from the tubes," Marie said.

"You had a brawl with some tubes," Jo said.

"Willie startled me, and I fell on them," Marie said, cleaning her blazer with a wet towel.

"I must admire your commitment to fetching those buns," Jo said, putting a hand on Marie's shoulder. "See you in ten minutes for the replanning of the town hall?"

Marie was five minutes late to their replanning meeting, but she had managed to wash the streaks off her blazer and dry it with the hand dryer. Her shoe still sparkled with sugar crystals, but she had managed to remove them from inside the shoe. When Marie arrived, the team was huddled in front of the whiteboard in the meeting room, already deep in discussion. On the whiteboard, the team had drawn the canteen and the tables in the canteen.

"If we divide the canteen into zones, we will only have to worry about five or six tables each," Eric said.

"We'll need to split some of the longer tables," Sheila said, pointing to the board, "otherwise we won't be able to re-mix the teams for the second round of discussions."

Within an hour, the team had written a detailed playbook of the town hall and assigned responsibilities to each of them.

Later that day, as Marie walked down to lunch, she met Eric on the stairwell.

"I've been wondering, Marie," he said, "why is only one of your shoes sparkling?"

Marie laughed and told him about her adventures in the basement earlier that morning. He looked concerned.

"Willie said he removed the buns Monday evening?" he asked.

"Yeah, I did find that weird," Marie said.

When they entered the canteen, Marie noticed Joseph walking from table to table, trailing his hand across the tabletops. People seated at the tables were looking at the palms of their hands. Lunch-goers who had not yet sat down were standing and holding their trays, looking around.

"What's going on?" Eric said.

Marie darted straight for Joseph. "Joseph," she shouted.

He looked at her. "It's sugar," he said, showing Marie the palm of his hand. "The tables are covered in sugar."

Marie looked at the table closest to her. It was sparkling like her shoe. She stroked it with her palm. It wasn't a lot of sugar. The layer was about one crystal thick and impossible to spot from a distance.

"It must have taken time to spread such a thin layer," Joseph said.

"When do you clean the tables?" Marie asked.

"It must have been done yesterday evening," Joseph said. "We clean the tables after lunch."

Marie looked at him.

"My staff leave at around five in the afternoon," Joseph said.

Suddenly, a realization hit Marie. "Joseph, I need to go talk to someone who was here last night," she said.

"Do you have a suspect?" he asked.

"Maybe a witness," she said, not wanting to jump to conclusions.

The kitchen staff started washing the tables. As Marie walked away, she heard Joseph mumble "Merda appiccicosa" under his breath. *Huh,* Marie thought, *he's Italian.*

Marie had almost reached the stairs when a few people in front of her suddenly ducked.

"Ah!" Marie exclaimed, hearing a thunderous sound and ducking, too.

After a few seconds of squatting on the floor with her arms over her head, she carefully looked up and saw that a banner had unfolded right above her and was hanging from the stairwell.

She took a couple of steps back to read the words written with black marker on the slightly stained cardboard banner: "YOU HAVE SUGAR ON YOUR HANDS."

At this point, Marie couldn't help herself. She burst into laughter. She laughed so hard she gasped for air but just couldn't stop. She felt someone put a hand on her shoulder and lead her out of the canteen. She looked to her right and saw Eric.

"What's gotten into you?" he asked.

Marie laughed even harder.

"Well … It's accurate …" she managed to say but then went back to laughing.

"We all have sugar on our hands," she finally said, showing Eric the palm of her hand.

Eric sat her down on the floor in the hallway and sat next to her. It took a couple of minutes before she stopped laughing. Then, her laughs were replaced by shivers. Eric took off his blazer and covered Marie with it.

"You're in shock," he said.

Marie nodded and huddled under his blazer. After a few more minutes, she stopped shaking. She took a deep breath.

"I think it's Willie," she finally said.

"Me too," Eric said.

"It's a bit elaborate for a practical joke," Marie said.

"The energy seems too pent up for this stunt to just be a joke," Eric agreed.

"It must have taken hours and hours to spread that sugar so thinly on all the tables in the canteen," Marie said.

"He would have had to remove the sugar from the pantry and tables little by little," Eric said.

"This has taken weeks of planning," Marie agreed.

"What's happened recently that could have prompted this?" Eric asked.

"Simon and Jason resigned," Marie said. "We've onboarded new people."

"We got the soda fridges," Eric said.

Marie looked at him. "Is that the sugar he's hinting at on the banner?" she wondered.

"Now that I think about it, all the soda in the fridge contains real sugar," Eric said.

"Natalie doesn't believe in artificial sweeteners," Marie said. "She's told me about her skepticism toward aspartame."

"But why would the soda fridges be so upsetting," Eric said, "regardless of the types of soda stocked?"

"We need to speak to Willie," Marie concluded.

Sweet Loyalty

Marie and Eric walked across the canteen toward the staircase. People were sitting and eating their lunch now. The banner was still up, and several people were looking at it. A couple of colleagues stopped and looked at Marie. She realized that she was still wearing Eric's blazer. She took it off.

As they went around the staircase to head down to the basement, they met Shaine, an engineer who previously worked at ConvoSystems, coming up. He smiled at Marie and Eric.

"What's for lunch today?" he asked as he passed them.

"Excitement," Marie said.

Raising an eyebrow, Shaine looked at her and walked toward the buffet. Marie and Eric walked down the stairwell.

"Why do you think Willie would be down here?" Eric asked.

"He was here last time I saw him," Marie said.

Eric shrugged. "Wouldn't he be in the data center?" he said.

Marie stopped walking. "You're probably right," she said. She thought for a moment. "But since we're here, I can show you the boxes of sugar I put my shoe through this morning," she said.

They continued down the stairwell, but when she got to the area where the boxes were earlier in the day, there were just server casings.

"They were right here," Marie said. "There were five of them."

Eric crouched and looked around. "There are some empty sugar packets here," he said.

They rummaged for a couple more minutes but found nothing else of interest.

As they headed back up the stairs, Shaine was heading down.

"What was for lunch?" Marie asked.

"Lasagna," Shaine said, "and a banner. Did you see that thing?"

"It almost fell on Marie as it unfolded," Eric said.

Shaine scoffed. "It's just a carton," he said. "There are loads of them in the corner of the basement."

Suddenly, Marie's stomach felt uneasy. "What are you doing in the basement, by the way?" she asked.

His eyes narrowed. "I could ask you the same thing," he said, perhaps jokingly.

"We were looking for boxes of sugar," Marie said. "I saw them this morning, but now they're gone."

Shaine smiled. "Jenni asked me to clear out the basement," he said. "I've been throwing stuff in the bins all morning."

"What did you do to earn such a harsh punishment?" Eric asked.

"I volunteered," he said. "We could use more storage space for spare parts for the data center. We just need to clear out the rubbish and put up shelves."

"I guess it could be a storage space," Eric said, looking around. "Simon wasn't the most well-organized person when he was in charge of the data center."

"Exactly," Shaine said, "and now it's time for a more well-organized person to step into that role."

"Have you seen Willie today?" Eric asked.

"I met him in the basement this morning," Shaine said. "I might have pissed him off. I gave him my frank opinion about his old boss Simon's leadership abilities."

"How did he react?" Marie asked.

"He was alright," Shaine said, "until I asked why he was still sticking around this dump of a company."

Marie could feel her fists tightening.

"Get it?" he said. "Because we were standing in the company dump."

"And what did he say to that?" she asked.

"He got the same look on his face as you have now," Shaine said, "but I told him that changing jobs is a smart move to get a higher salary."

Eric and Marie looked at Shaine.

"That's when he got cross and stormed out," Shaine continued.

"That's it?" Eric said. "You didn't say anything else to him?"

Shaine looked at his feet. "I might have told him how much I made at ConvoSystems and how much I'm making here," he said.

Marie looked at him. "We encourage transparency about salary levels," Marie finally said, mostly to herself.

"Maybe you shouldn't," Shaine said, "or maybe you shouldn't be paying someone double what others make." He turned on his heel and headed downstairs.

Now Marie noticed a roll of black trash bags sticking out of the back pocket of his jeans. He really was ready to clear out the basement.

Marie looked at Eric. "Do we really pay Shaine double the salary we pay Willie?" she asked Eric.

"We would need to ask Paul," Eric said. "He's in charge of making offers and ensuring fair salary bands."

Eric excused himself to go to a meeting. Marie considered whether to go for lunch or head back up to her office. She wasn't hungry. She had almost reached her office when she heard Mark calling from behind.

"Hey," he said, "are you OK? I heard that banner almost hit you."

"Yeah, I'm fine," she said, "but I couldn't stop laughing for a couple minutes."

"You got a serious fright then," he said.

"It's better now," she said, "but I do want to find Willie."

"Willie?" Mark said. "Why?"

"Let's sit in my office," Marie said.

They both went inside, and Marie closed the door behind her. Then she suddenly realized something.

"Oh shoot," she said, "we were supposed to start brainstorming CFO recruitment an hour ago. I completely forgot! Eric and I were in the basement looking for boxes of sugar."

Mark squinted at her. "Boxes of sugar," he said. "Why were you looking for sugar? It seems like we have an excess of sugar currently."

Marie explained to him how she met Willie in the basement that morning and how Joseph had noticed sugar going missing. She even showed him her glittering shoe as evidence.

He sat back in her armchair. "You left a bag of cinnamon buns in the basement for a whole week," he said, making a whistling sound. "I thought you were a perfectionist."

She knew he was kidding. But she was not in the mood.

"I think it's Willie," she said, "and that it has something to do with the soda machines ... or maybe his salary compared to Shaine's." Then she realized something. Mark was involved in the hiring process, too. "Is it true that we pay Shaine double what we pay Willie?" she asked.

He thought for a minute. "Probably not exactly double," he said, "but thereabouts."

Marie could feel the ball of lava boiling over in her gut. "Why? Why would we pay a complete newcomer double the amount that we pay an employee who has been with us from the very beginning?" she almost shouted.

"Because he's unlikely to leave," Mark said calmly. "Willie is very loyal to Zebra. He's shown us that time and time again."

Marie was about to shout something else. Instead, she held it in and looked sternly at Mark.

He looked back at her. Then down. "We had to poach Shaine from ConvoSystems," Mark said. "The only way was to offer him significantly higher pay."

Marie kept looking at him without making a sound.

"Jenni was really short on people," Mark continued. "We had to find someone to backfill for Simon."

"Double," Marie said.

"Or thereabouts," Mark said.

"After everything that Willie has done for us," Marie continued.

Mark shifted in his seat. "Now, we've done a lot for Willie, too," he said. "We paid to retrain him. We paid for his degree and gave him paid time off to pursue his studies."

"Yes, but he kept doing his janitorial work on top of his new responsibilities until we found his replacement," Marie said. "He has been nothing but …" she stopped herself.

"Loyal?" Mark said.

Was this really what Zebra had become? Marie thought. *Didn't loyalty to the company mean anything? Were we more concerned about filling headcount than creating a sustainable team to carry the company forward?*

"Who gave him the offer?" Marie asked.

"Paul," Mark said. "Based on his salary band matrix, like all the other offers we present."

Marie got up from her office chair.

Mark looked up at her. "Do you really think Willie wrote the banner?" he asked her.

"We won't know until we ask him, will we?" she said through her teeth.

"Marie," Mark said.

Marie kept standing and looking at her door.

"Marie," Mark repeated.

She looked at him.

"Let's go to my office and brainstorm CFO candidates," he said.

Ignoring Mark, Marie grabbed her bag from beside her table and rushed out the door. Only when she was in her car in the parking lot did Marie realize she had left her phone and laptop in her office. She thought about going back up there but couldn't make a single muscle in her body move. She couldn't believe Mark. For weeks now, she had seen another side of him. A side that she had come to appreciate, even like. This time, the lava inside her stomach stung even more than before. Knowing that he could be different but wasn't consistently being so. She turned the key in the ignition and drove home.

It's You Or Me

On Wednesday morning, Ally woke up with a fever, and Marie decided to stay home with her. She felt like she needed a break from work anyhow. Since she had forgotten her phone and laptop on her desk, she couldn't work even if she had wanted to. Ally lay exhausted on the couch, watching Peppa Pig under a blanket. Marie sat beside her and looked out the window at the birds flying in and out of the birdhouse.

Suddenly, Marie heard a ringing. Ally lifted her head for a moment, then put it back down on her pillow. Marie stroked her cheek and got up to walk toward the sound. It was Eric FaceTiming her on her iPad.

"Clever workaround," she said, answering the call.

"Mark came by and gave me your phone," Eric said, "so I figured I'd need to find another way to reach you."

"What's wrong with having a child's sick day?" Marie said.

"I've spoken to Willie," Eric said.

"Where was he?" Marie asked.

"He was in the data center this morning," Eric said. "On time for his shift."

"He is very ..." Marie said, but she didn't want to continue.

"Loyal," Eric said.

Somehow, that word would have tasted like ashes in Marie's mouth.

"He said that it all started with a couple of sugar packets," Eric said.

"He admitted that it was him?" Marie asked.

"It's less planned than we assumed, though," Eric said. "He said it started with him ripping sugar packets at lunchtime whenever he felt stressed. Since no one was using the sugar anyway, he felt like it didn't do any harm."

"Where would he put the sugar?" Marie asked.

"He would just rip the packet and pour the sugar on his plate before bussing it," Eric said.

"That seems pretty harmless," Marie said.

"Then Shaine joined the company," Eric continued, "and he is ... well ..."

"A jerk," Marie said.

Eric laughed. "He sure acts like one," he said. "Willie started taking packets of sugar to rip in the afternoon since he and Shaine work in the data center together after lunch."

"Would he rip them in the data center?" Marie asked.

"No, he would rip them in the basement during his afternoon break—ripping more and more until he eventually filled the boxes that you put your foot through," Eric said.

"Ripping the sugar packets was a kind of stress release for Willie to help him deal with an uncomfortable relationship," Marie said.

"Yeah," Eric said, "but then he made his way through all the sugar from the canteen tables and ended up with all this sugar in boxes."

"Did he take the sugar from the pantry too?" Marie asked.

"I didn't ask about that specifically," Eric said, "but he didn't have a plan for what to do with the sugar."

"Did Shaine do something to push him over the edge?" Marie asked.

"Did you know that Willie has diabetes?" Eric asked back.

"No, I didn't know that," Marie said.

"When Mark had the soda fridges installed," Eric said, "Willie felt excluded from the benefits that the company was providing."

"It does have something to do with the soda!" Marie exclaimed.

"And when he learned that Shaine was being compensated way more than him, he just felt like the company wasn't taking care of him anymore," Eric continued.

Marie went quiet.

"He didn't do anything illegal," Eric went on.

"He did vandalize the canteen," Marie said.

"That's why I'm calling," Eric said. "I need you to speak to Mark and Paul."

"They'll decide what we do about this behavior," Marie thought aloud.

"You need to make sure that they see Willie's point of view," Eric said.

"Do they know that you've spoken to Willie?" Marie asked.

"No, and I asked Willie to avoid our floor for today," he said.

"I'll figure out a way to come in," Marie said and hung up.

She FaceTimed Thomas' mother, who agreed to come over and look after Ally that afternoon. Then Marie changed out of her gray sweatpants and into her red pantsuit.

Ally mustered all her energy to get off the couch and hug her grandma when she came an hour later.

As Marie pulled out of her driveway, what had started out as a strong sense of purpose suddenly felt flaccid. *What was she going to say to Paul?* She thought back to her conversation with Anne at the coffee shop—how Anne had accused Marie of crowding out Paul's initiative. Paul had withdrawn into his own HR operations silo. Marie stayed out of operations, and Paul stayed out of anything that wasn't operations.

They didn't even greet each other in the hallway. There were no HR leadership meetings. Mark spoke to them separately.

She parked in front of the office. For a couple of minutes, she sat staring at the steering wheel without moving. She turned off the engine, took a deep breath, and thought, *I'll just have to wing it,* as she opened the car door.

When Marie knocked on his door, Paul looked up at her from behind his monitor, his glasses almost sliding down his nose.

"We need to talk," Marie said, closing the door behind her.

"Can we …" Paul started but stopped when he noticed Marie looking sternly at him.

"OK," Paul said, "let's talk."

He pushed the glasses up his nose and leaned back in his chair. Marie sat in the chair across from him. He opened his mouth to say something, but Marie beat him to it.

"Why are we paying Shaine double the amount we're paying Willie?" Marie asked.

Paul yanked his head back and furrowed his eyebrows—clearly not expecting this topic.

"Listen, Marie, I can't remember everyone's compensation by heart," he said. "I can have Esther look into it."

He stood up and pointed toward the door.

Marie stayed in her chair.

He sat back down and looked at her. "What is this about?" he asked.

"It's about your principles, Paul," Marie said.

Paul rolled his eyes. "My principles," he said. He looked at her and put his elbows on the table. "It's about you not being able to mind your own damn business," he said in a low tone. "Here comes Marie to the rescue of some poor employee being mistreated by HR," he said, shifting his pitch up.

This was the first time Paul had said anything remotely nonmechanical to her. She wasn't about to let this thaw go to waste.

"Are you HR in this scenario?" she asked. "Mistreating employees."

He clenched his jaw and tightened his fist. "What do you want?" he asked, now in his regular tone.

"I want to have a conversation with my colleague, Paul," she said, "not the HR operations automaton."

"Automaton," he said and threw his hands in the air. "Get out, Marie."

"No," Marie said. "We've feuded long enough, and our lack of collaboration is hurting employees."

He shifted in his seat and started looking at the door behind Marie.

"I understand I've stepped on your toes," Marie said.

"That's an understatement," Paul said, turning away from her.

"Well, tell me the real statement," Marie said. "You've never told me how I made you feel."

"That's something you touchy-feely guys in HR development have time for," Paul said, waving his hand in Marie's direction. "I have a company to run."

He turned toward his monitor and started tapping on his keyboard.

Marie stood up and hovered over his screen.

"Paul," she said, "I've optimized many HR operations in my time as a consultant. I can do your job." He looked up at her. "You cannot do mine. I can ask Mark to pick who he wants to keep," she said, crossing her arms.

"How dare you," he said as he stood up.

"You can either work with me to resolve our issues," she said, opening her arms, "or you can be history."

At that, Paul stormed out and headed straight for Mark's office.

Marie sat back down in the chair across from Paul's desk. *I didn't see that one coming,* she thought, her mind now completely blank.

A minute later, Eric walked by the door. Seeing Marie in Paul's office, he walked backward and popped his head through the doorway.

"Marie," he said, "what are you doing in Paul's office—without Paul?"

"Pissing him off," Marie said.

"Yeah, I just saw him in Mark's office," he said. "He seemed rather animated." Eric looked at Marie. "Come on, let's get you reunited with your phone," he said.

Marie stood up and followed Eric to his desk. They passed Mark's office on the way, and Mark looked at

Marie through the glass next to his door. Marie met his gaze but had a hard time reading his expression. He seemed to have a sparkle in his eye.

"Any more news on Willie?" Marie asked Eric.

"No, he's been in the data center most of the day," Eric said. He looked at Marie. "Have you spoken to Paul or Mark about him yet?"

"Apparently, I've chosen to address the underlying issue of how we put Willie in the position he's in rather than talking about Willie directly," Marie said, shrugging.

"That might be a smart approach," Eric said.

"'Might' being the operative word," Marie said.

"You've got this, Marie," Eric said.

Marie looked at him and tried to smile, but her stomach had stiffened into what felt like concrete.

She was trying to focus on reading emails in her office when Mark walked in. He closed the door behind him, looked at her, and whistled.

"Are we in a mood today?" he said.

She looked at him, trying to read his intention. His eyes were still sparkling.

"What do you mean?" she said as calmly as she could muster.

"I told you I wanted to do a museum of failure session with you and Paul," he said. "Seems like you've already started digging up corpses." His expression was soft, and he seemed cheerful.

"Willie is getting caught in the middle of our HR dysfunction," Marie said.

"Because of his salary gap with Shaine?" Mark asked.

"And because of the freaking soda machines," Marie said.

Mark rolled his eyes. "Everyone is on my case about those soda machines," he said.

"They make no sense," Marie said. "What were you thinking?"

Mark's expression toughened. He looked at the floor. "I wasn't doing my best work," he said. He looked at Marie. "We're not the only group with dysfunction. I'm not sure you understand the pressure I face."

Marie nodded. She didn't understand.

"We need to mend the relationship between you and Paul," he said.

Now Marie nodded.

"You don't understand the pressures he faces either," Mark said.

Marie lifted her eyebrows.

"You don't deal with the legal issues we have sometimes," Mark continued, "and Paul has had a really tough month after the Frank situation."

"Did Frank sue us?" she asked.

"No. We let Frank go," Mark said.

Marie straightened in her seat. "I thought he resigned," she said. Then, a thought struck her—if Frank was let go, his leaving wasn't Sheila's fault. The thought made her smile.

Mark interrupted her thoughts, "As I said, it's been a really difficult month for Paul."

The block of ice in Marie's gut suddenly thawed. "I had no idea," she said.

"You're right about one thing," Mark said. "Paul mentioned you think our dysfunction is hurting employees. But it's not just from Paul's side—and threatening him with dismissal isn't going to solve it."

"You're also right that I would pick you if I had to choose," Mark said, smiling.

"You probably shouldn't tell me that," Marie said.

"Why not?" he said as he leaned back. "You already know. But you can't do both jobs at the same time. I would rather you focus on developing our organization than running it."

She looked at him. What was this expression on his face? Pride? Caring?

"We need to solve the dysfunction between you and Paul," he said, "but we're going to do it in the right way."

"We do need to talk about Willie, though," Marie said.

"He pulled the sugar stunt, didn't he?" Mark said.

"Yes, but it's not his fault," Marie said. "We've dropped the ball with him."

"I figured you were trying to protect someone, acting out like that," Mark said.

Marie could feel her cheeks heating up. Was she that transparent?

"Let's give Willie a free pass on this one while we clean up our own mess," Mark said.

"Just like that?" Marie asked.

"I am the VP of HR," Mark said and got up to leave.

The Town Hall

On Thursday morning, Marie found Willie waiting for her in the parking lot. As soon as Marie slammed the car door, Willie approached her.

"Do I need to stay in the server room today, too?" he asked.

Marie smiled. "No, you can go wherever you want," Marie said.

Willie nodded. "What will happen to me?" he asked.

"Eventually, justice," Marie said.

Willie's eyes widened. "Will I be fired?" he asked.

Marie chuckled. "No, not justice for the sugar incident," Marie clarified. "Justice for being grossly underpaid."

Willie looked down at the asphalt.

Marie continued, "Mark isn't going to pursue this incident. It's not on you—it's a broader problem."

"That's not fair either," Willie said. "You don't see other employees freaking out like that."

Marie looked at him. "Which other employees do you mean?" she asked.

"The engineers," he said. "You know—in Jenni's team."

"Why would they need to freak out?" Marie said.

"Well, they don't freak out," Willie said.

"But why should they?" Marie asked.

"Because of the pay disparities," Willie continued. "Everyone hired in the past year makes almost double the more seasoned team members."

Marie's jaw dropped. "What?" she almost shouted.

"I thought you knew," Willie said.

"I … I …" Marie stammered.

"But I'm off the hook?" Willie said.

"Yeah," Marie said, thinking that she clearly was not off the hook yet.

As Marie walked toward her office, she heard loud laughter coming from inside. It was the rolling giggles of Sheila. Marie smiled. It was comforting to hear Sheila in a good mood. Marie opened the door to her office.

"Is there a party in here?" she asked.

"Town hall today," Sheila said, "and we'll be ready!"

"We'll be overprepared," Jo said in a flat tone.

Marie looked at her and raised an eyebrow.

"But we're being really supportive of Sheila's need to prepare," Jo went on, equally flat.

Sheila put her arm around Jo. "I know you're hating me a little bit right now."

"I don't hate you," Jo said, "I'm just bored of this already. We've gone over it ten times this morning. You know exactly how it's going to go down. Plus, you had nothing to worry about in the first place."

"How about we take Marie through it one last time?" Eric said.

Sheila went on to explain the plan for the day to Marie.

"And how do we close?" Marie asked once Sheila had finished.

"When the second bell rings, you'll get up on the podium and explain that we'll be taking everyone's input and converting it into actionable notes," Sheila said, "and that we'll visit their individual department meetings to discuss the notes."

"I told you you've got it," Jo said.

"Let's go rearrange the tables and put out the name tags," Eric said.

"Does Joseph know that we'll be rearranging the seating in the canteen?" Marie asked.

Eric, Jo, and Sheila looked at each other.

"Let's go tell him now," Sheila said, heading out of the office. Eric and Jo followed suit.

The canteen was buzzing a couple of minutes before the town hall was about to start. Marie was standing on the podium, looking at the top of the stairs. The banner had been taken down. Her hands were sweaty. How many engineers were as dissatisfied as Willie but didn't have the creativity to put up a banner to let everyone know?

Jo came over and gave Marie a microphone. Natalie was pacing below the podium while speaking on the phone. Natalie got off the phone and gave it to Jo.

"Dear colleagues," Marie started. The room was still buzzing noisily. "Dear colleagues," Marie went on. Now, the room was falling silent. "We have a special edition of the town hall for you today, where we will work through our values and what they mean for how we work. First, here is Natalie to reintroduce our company values."

People started clapping. As Marie handed Natalie the microphone, Jo turned on the slide that showed the company's values.

Natalie went on to tell the story of how the company was founded and how she and Richard had set out to make learning better for children and more dignified for teachers.

Marie was looking around the room. At one of the tables, an animated discussion was happening. Marie slowly walked over to Jo and whispered, "How have you distributed people at the tables for the first round?"

"Mainly by department," Jo said.

"Who is sitting at that table on the left?" Marie asked.

"Those are engineers," Jo said, "from both the data center and the development teams."

Marie's heart sank. There they were—the engineers who were equally as unhappy as Willie.

Sitting together at a table, listening to the CEO of the company talking about the value of commitment. She slowly walked over to their table. She sat between the two most animated men. They both looked up at her, raising their eyebrows. One of them scooted over to the side. The other looked sternly at Marie.

"What are you, our kindergarten teacher?" he said, not bothering to whisper at all.

"Are you a child?" she retorted.

He laughed. "Alright, Marie, it's about time you made your way to engineering," he said.

She smiled at him as people started clapping at the end of Natalie's introduction. Jo introduced the first assignment from the stage. An engineer at the other end of the table started taking notes. Everyone at the table was discussing the assignment except the two engineers Marie was sitting next to.

"So, Marie, what does the value of commitment mean to you?" the engineer on her left asked. The one on her right moved in closer.

"That's the question posed to you," she said.

"No," the engineer on her right said, "because I understand commitment. I understand what it takes to deliver our solutions to the children who use them. I understand which servers ASLO lives on and how it's backed up. I understand because I built it myself. I understand because I spend my nights and weekends making sure that it keeps running. What do you understand? Sitting there on the second floor, poaching useless engineers who don't even know how to code from other companies. You're paying them twice our salary for contributing zero. Zero!"

Marie's cheeks started to flame.

The engineer stood up, threw his chair on the floor, and turned to Marie. "Zero!" he shouted and went for the door.

Marie swallowed, took a deep breath, and looked at the engineer on her left. "Do you feel the same way?" she asked, her voice cracking.

"He's a drama queen," he said. "No, I've got my résumé all polished up. I'm taking a note out of Natalie's book on what commitment means at Zebra Apps." He crossed his arms and sat back in his chair.

Marie didn't know what to do.

"Come with me," a voice said from behind Marie.

Marie turned around to see the CTO, Jenni, standing behind her. They walked into the hallway, where Jenni stopped.

"You got Willie off the hook?" Jenni said.

"There were bigger things at play," Marie said.

Jenni looked down. Marie looked at her. Her eyes were puffy, her lips dry, and her hair was unevenly split. "How are you, Jenni?" she asked.

Jenni looked up and sighed. "You just sat next to how I am," she said. "It's borderline mutiny."

"In the engineering department?" Marie asked.

"Everyone wants higher pay, and the old guard isn't letting any of the new employees near customer-facing assignments," Jenni said.

"Seems like they feel overlooked," Marie said.

"No shit, Marie," Jenni said and rolled her eyes.

Marie furrowed her eyebrows.

"I'm sorry," Jenni said, "but you've just witnessed five minutes of what I face every damn day."

"How long has it been like this?" Marie asked.

"Since Shaine started," she said. "He's a piece of work."

"A well-paid one," Marie said.

"But it was probably already like this before. Shaine just pushed everyone over the edge," Jenni said. "It's like he pushed the human system out of equilibrium," she added, mostly to herself.

Jenni looked at Marie. "You sound like Anne," she said.

"Anyway," Jenni said, "I need you to work your HR magic on the engineering team."

"What do you have in mind?" Marie asked.

"I won't tell you how to do your job," Jenni said, "just fix my team."

Marie thought for a moment. "OK. Let's fix your team," she said finally.

Jenni went back to the canteen to rejoin the town hall. Marie was about to go inside too but saw Paul walking out. She followed him.

"Hey Paul," she shouted, almost sprinting to catch up with him.

He turned around. "Not now, Marie," he said.

"It's always 'not now' with you," she said in the lightest tone she could muster.

He turned around and stopped. "There's nothing wrong with your little workshop; that's not why I'm leaving," he said.

"Then why are you leaving 'my little workshop'?" Marie said, making air quotes with her fingers.

"I'm due in court," he said and started walking again.

"Jury duty," she concluded to herself.

He turned around and stopped again. "No. Today, we start the lawsuit against Frank," he said, this time staying long enough to wait for her reaction.

"Why are we suing Frank?" she asked.

"Because of what happened with Andrea," he said. Marie could swear that there was a momentary smile on his face as he said it.

"Why? What happened with Andrea?" she asked.

"Let's say Frank didn't handle things well," Paul said, turned around and walked away.

Marie didn't go after him. *How did I miss these events?* she thought. At that moment, she heard the timer ding in the canteen, indicating that the next round of discussions was about to begin.

Skeletons And Corpses

Mark was insistent—Mark, Paul, and Marie were to spend a whole day together at an offsite at a seaside hotel. They had only one item on the agenda: the museum of failure.

Paul was pouring himself a cup of coffee when Marie found him. His eyes were puffy, and he was pale. He extended his hand toward Marie. She shook it.

"So formal this morning," Marie said.

Paul shrugged and picked up his coffee cup.

"How is the hearing going?" Marie asked.

Paul shook his head. "Don't mention it," he said.

"Late night yesterday?" Marie asked.

"Every night's a late night these days," Paul said, "and now Mark wants to take a full day out to 'dust off the skeletons.'"

Marie smirked. "Is that how he explained it?" Marie asked.

"What did he tell you?" Paul asked.

"That we're going to do the museum of failure exercise together," Marie said.

Paul narrowed his eyes. "I already know that you left a bag of cinnamon buns at the bottom of the stairwell for two weeks," he said with a gentle smile.

Marie laughed. "Wait a minute now, it was only one week," she said.

"I never pictured you as someone who would overlook something like that," he said. "You're always perfect."

"I'm far from perfect," Marie said, "and these days, I'm finding out the magnitude of things I've been overlooking. Like whatever's happening with Frank's court case."

"You know I can't really discuss that," Paul said.

"But is there anything I should be catching with Andrea?" Marie said.

"Let's focus on getting her a fair hearing in court," Paul said.

I can't really use the bun incident again, Marie thought as she made her way to the conference room. Then, she noticed that the hallway was decorated with pictures of Ukrainian families. Several pictures showed the Ukrainian flag—wrapped around people or as blue and yellow streamers glued around the frames. This made Marie think back to the flower party at Ally's kindergarten and how she had forgotten to buy streamers because she spent the afternoon with Anne instead. *That would be safe to share,* Marie thought.

Mark was already in the conference room. He had put a gray-brown sheet of cardboard on the wall and written the rules of the museum of failure exercise on the whiteboard. The tables in the room were pushed against the walls, so there was an open floor space in the middle.

Paul entered the room.

"Great, we're all here," Mark said.

"You've forgotten the mead," Paul said.

Marie laughed.

"I didn't think it was appropriate this early in the morning," Mark said.

"How will we celebrate our mistakes, then?" Marie asked, playfully looking over at Paul. He met her gaze with a smile.

"Jo said that there are no rules," Mark said. "We can decide what counts as a celebration."

"Is this really the only thing we have on our agenda today?" Paul asked.

"Yes," Mark said with a smile, "today we're digging up all the corpses."

"Not only do we have skeletons but corpses, too," Marie said.

"You can't just force it," Paul said.

"Digging up all the corpses is a little ambitious," Marie said. "Maybe let's aim to get a bit more closely aligned."

"Completely agree," Paul said.

Marie looked at Paul. This was the most agreeing the two of them had ever done.

Mark kicked off the exercise by sharing an incident where he parked in an accessible parking space next to a pharmacy and found a parking ticket under his windscreen wiper after he'd picked up the medicine.

"Now, *that* is poor judgment," Paul said.

"What if I told you that my then two-year-old son was burning up with fever, and my wife had gone into labor that same evening," Mark said, his pupils dilating.

"I would have done the exact same thing," Marie said.

"Me too," Paul said quietly.

Mark sat down. "I wouldn't have done anything differently," he said.

"It's not really a mistake, is it?" Paul said. "It's a calculated risk. And an ancient one at that—your daughter is fourteen."

"She's thirteen," Mark said.

"So, you brought us on this retreat, made us take a whole day out of our calendars," Paul said, "to dust off skeletons and dig up corpses, and the only thing you're sharing is a non-mistake from thirteen years ago."

Marie was baffled. Her relationship with Mark wasn't great, but it seemed that Paul's was even worse.

"This counts as starting small," Marie said. "It says something about HR leadership at our company that even the boss doesn't feel safe to disclose any weakness," she went on.

Paul threw his hands up in the air. "Why can't we just do our jobs?" he said. "I don't have time for this bullshit."

"Because we're not doing our jobs," Mark said. "I know that I'm not. I got the soda fridges installed."

"That's a perk," Paul said.

"That's a lazy perk," Mark said, "and I knew that when I signed the work order. I couldn't have known it would push Willie over the edge and go full-on sugar-gate on us, but I knew it wouldn't lead to better employee satisfaction."

"Why did you do it, then?" Marie asked.

"To do something," Mark said. "Anything."

Paul crossed his arms. "Both Esther and I had to work late for a week to figure out the tax implications of that," he said, "and you're telling me you initiated it knowing it wouldn't work?"

"Why would it take a whole week to figure out how to tax soda?" Marie asked.

Paul looked her up and down. "And you say that you can do my job."

Marie raised her eyebrows and looked at Mark. "Why did you feel like you had to do something?" she asked him.

"Because people were leaving Zebra Apps," he said. "I'd seen the trend for the past year, but I didn't care enough to even bring it up with Natalie."

"Why didn't you care in the first place?" Marie asked.

"Because it wouldn't matter anyway," Mark said. "I've been fighting Natalie to focus on our culture ever since I started. She pays lip service, but she's so afraid that the company will fail that she'll jump at any commercial opportunity and avoid financial risk at any price."

"Why do you stay then?" Paul asked.

Mark looked at Paul. Then back at Marie. "I like what we've built together," he said.

"Paul, you're a savant when it comes to contracts, taxes, and salaries," Mark said. "I never have to worry about our legal and financial platform."

He looked at Marie. "And you care so deeply about our leaders and our people that you're willing to poke at any skeleton," he paused, "or dig up any corpse to protect Willie. We're the best HR team I've ever worked with."

Marie looked at him. He was still wearing a half-smile on his face.

"Except that we're not a team," Paul said.

"Agreed," Marie said, "we're the most non-team I've ever been a part of."

"That's my biggest mistake," Mark said. "Not having invested in making us a team. That's why we're here today—to rectify my mistake."

The room went quiet for a couple of moments. Paul looked over at the brownish poster.

"You appear to have missed a step. Was that a bad outcome or a lapse in judgment?" Paul asked, with a smile on his face.

They continued to complete Mark's mistake-sharing and toasted with coffee while shouting, "To hell with it." Mark drew a Post-it showing three smiling stick figures and added it to the poster.

Paul shared how he made a taxation error when it came to taxing the vehicles that some members of their sales team were allotted. Marie lost her concentration a couple of times while Paul was explaining the intricacies of what happened. He celebrated his mistake with high fives.

After lunch, it was Marie's turn to share.

"Well," Marie said, "there is this other mother at my daughter Ally's kindergarten who would probably tell you that I'm failing as a mother." Marie intended it to be a joke, but neither Paul nor Mark pulled a muscle.

Marie suddenly felt exposed. "I'm not actually failing as a mother," she said.

"Say more about why this other mother might think so," Paul said.

Marie looked at the door. Then she looked out the window. She took a deep breath. "A month ago, we had a flower party at my daughter's kindergarten. I'm part of the party committee, and I was supposed to bring the decorations. But I got distracted and forgot all about it," Marie said. "Carrie's mom had bought decorations herself, so even though I forgot them, the party went ahead as planned."

"Why didn't she just agree to buy them in the first place?" Paul asked.

"Because she's testing me," Marie said, shrugging. "You see, at the previous party, I forgot to bring sprinkles for the cake."

"And what happened at that party?" Mark asked.

"We lost a cake competition, and Carrie's mom blamed me," Marie said.

Mark raised his eyebrows.

"The cake did get eaten. And it was all for a good cause," Marie said. "To raise money for a new playground."

"How did you feel about forgetting the decorations?" Paul asked.

Marie thought for a minute. "It made me feel like I wasn't playing my part—like I wasn't being a proper parent." She looked at Paul. "But when I think about it, it makes no sense," Marie continued. "Why should my parenting be judged by my ability to remember to bring things to parties at kindergarten?"

"I forgot to bring my son's birthday cake to his kindergarten once," Paul said. "On his actual birthday. I only remembered when we got to his classroom. The door to the classroom was decorated with flags and his picture. My heart sank. I'd forgotten the cake at home on the kitchen counter, and there was no time to go back for it. We were in the middle of closing the books on the financial year at my previous company."

"Did you feel like a bad parent?" Marie asked.

"Like the worst," Paul said, "even though my son didn't care at the time. He was three. It was more the comments from the teachers at kindergarten."

"What did they say?" Mark asked.

"They said things like 'We all know that you have an important job' and 'Next time, how about Felicia makes the cake arrangements,'" Paul said. "Felicia is my wife."

"I hate when that happens," Mark said. "I don't know how many times my kids' teachers have called me to talk about the kids and said, 'Oh, we didn't realize it was your number, Mark; we'll try Elizabeth instead.' Like I'm some second-tier parent."

"Even though you forget sprinkles and decorations, Marie, you're still the default parent," Paul said.

"But no one expects you to volunteer for cake competitions," Marie said.

"I wish they did," Paul said. "I bake the best cakes. And my wife can't even follow a recipe."

Marie studied his face. He was completely earnest.

"I'm serious," Paul said, "I'm a really good baker."

Mark and Marie laughed.

"I'll prove it to you," Paul said. "I'll bake cinnamon buns for next Friday's breakfast."

"You'll come to Friday breakfast?" Marie asked.

"If you serve my buns, I will," Paul said.

Marie extended her hand toward Paul. He shook it.

"What distracted you?" Mark asked Marie.

Marie looked at Mark.

"I mean, when you were supposed to buy decorations for Ally's party?" Mark clarified. "You usually remember everything. What made you forget them?"

"I'd planned to buy the streamers right before the party," Marie said, "but instead, I spent the afternoon with Anne."

"Anne?" Mark said, with his eyes wide.

Mark and Paul exchanged glances.

"Marie," Paul said, "Anne may not have the best interests of our company in mind."

Paul and Mark exchanged glances again.

"What?" Marie asked.

"She was let go," Mark said, finally.

"What?" Marie said. "Why would we let her go? She created our most successful products."

"She wasn't contributing," Paul said.

"Not contributing!" Marie almost shouted. "She was keeping the damn engineering department together. It's gone completely bonkers since she left."

"She wasn't contributing to the harmony of Zebra Apps," Mark said.

Marie looked at him. In her stomach, the familiar ball of lava was starting to boil. She felt her hands tighten into fists. "What harmony, Mark?" she said.

Mark looked at the carpet.

"Marie, you don't have the full picture," he said. "We let her go but knew how it would look. We didn't want the entire engineering department to walk out after her. Anne didn't want that either. We made an agreement with her that she would resign instead. We always expected that she might be back to meddle, and now it seems like she has indeed been meddling through you."

Marie suddenly felt dizzy. Was she being used by Anne? She thought that Anne had been trying to help.

"I need to be in court in forty-five minutes," Paul said. "I don't want to get stuck in traffic."

Mark nodded. Paul walked out the door. Mark drew a cake on a Post-it and hung it on the poster. He looked at Marie.

"Be careful," he said.

Yesterday's Board

It was 8:30 a.m. on Monday, and Marie was standing in front of a whiteboard on wheels in the hallway of the engineering department. As she waited, the lights turned off. She waved her hands to re-initiate them. She checked her watch again: 8:40 a.m. She checked her phone—daily scrum was scheduled for 8:30 a.m. every morning. Jenni had forwarded the invitation to Marie so that she could get a better sense of what was happening in the engineering team. *Nothing is happening,* she thought.

Marie took a closer look at the board. It was divided into sections, with Post-its in every section. Marie looked closer at an orange Post-it in the "Waiting for" section. It said "Calendar synchronization." *Wait a minute,* Marie thought; *ASLO already integrates with all commonly used calendars*. Then, it dawned on Marie. This board was old.

Marie walked down the hallway to find the engineers. She opened the door to one of the offices and saw five developers sitting at their desks with headphones on, looking intently at their screens. No one looked up. Marie looked around the room until one of the developers finally looked up and took his headphones off. She recognized him as one of the engineers she sat beside during the town hall.

"Oh, hey," she said. She looked at the tray on this desk for his name. "Ibrahim," she added.

He looked at the tray, too, and raised an eyebrow.

"We're in the middle of our daily scrum," he said.

"Staring at your screens?" she asked.

"Yeah," he said, "this way, Jenni can listen in on any of the teams. Today, she's with us."

"Is that your board in the hallway?" she asked.

Ibrahim looked in the direction Marie was pointing.

"It was," he said. "Everything's in Jira now."

Marie raised a questioning eyebrow.

"It's like a virtual board," he said, "that can also automate stuff."

"Cool," she said.

Ibrahim nodded, but his smile was stiff.

"How can I join in on your daily scrum?" Marie asked.

"Do you have the meeting link?" Ibrahim asked.

Marie nodded.

"Then you just join from there," Ibrahim said, "but we're almost done."

Marie looked at his screen. She could see Jenni's video. Jenni was muted and seemed to be typing away. The feed disappeared as everyone hung up.

Ibrahim looked at Marie. "So, you're the reason Jenni has graced us with her presence today?" he said.

Marie could feel the blood flowing to her face. "I guess I am," she said. "Jenni asked me to 'work my HR magic.'"

Another developer looked up. "God knows that's what we need," he said.

Marie looked at him, trying to understand if he was being ironic.

"Are you trying to read my tray, too?" the developer asked.

Ibrahim laughed. "That's Dennis," he said.

"It stings, Marie," Dennis said. "I've been at this company way longer than you have."

"I'm sorry," Marie said. "I'll make an effort to learn your names."

"He's messing with you," Ibrahim said.

Marie looked at Dennis. Then, back to Ibrahim. She had no idea who was messing with her. But one of them was.

"May I ask who your scrum master is?" Marie asked Ibrahim.

"We don't have one," Ibrahim said. "Never needed one."

"But who facilitates your ceremonies?" she asked.

"When we used to stand at the board, no one did. We all knew the drill and got through whatever needed to be discussed," he said. Then he thought for a minute. "Everyone who's been here from the beginning, at least those of us taught by Richard."

"How do you teach new people how to participate in your ceremonies, then?" Marie asked.

"We don't," he said. "They pick it up eventually."

Ibrahim started looking at his screen again. Marie felt it was time to go.

"I'll try to join your daily tomorrow," she said.

Ibrahim nodded.

Marie was about to go, but then she turned around. "Why is everyone so quiet?" she asked.

"Jenni wants us to be 'productive,'" Dennis said, making air quotes.

"That means no 'messy' stand-ups in the hallways," the developer by the window chimed in.

"And everyone needs to sit at their desks and code, code, code," Ibrahim said without looking up.

Marie raised both eyebrows.

"We miss Anne," Dennis added.

As Marie and Eric were having lunch later that day, she said, "Did you know that our developers aren't allowed to do in-person daily scrums standing at actual boards?"

Eric laughed and abruptly stopped when Marie's facial expression didn't change.

"That's when they're supposed to discuss all the issues," Eric said.

"Yeah, none of the developers were saying anything," Marie said, "and Jenni attended their daily scrum."

"Who will dare to air their dirtiest laundry if their manager is there?" Eric said.

"I wonder if all the teams are like this," Marie said.

"You could try asking Willie if the hardware team is any different," Eric suggested.

Marie put her knife and fork on her plate. "You know, I think I will," she said. She took her tray and left Eric to finish lunch on his own.

Marie found Willie in the break room near the data center.

"Hey, Marie," he said, "what are you doing in my dungeon?"

"Is it a dungeon now?" she said with a giggle.

"This is where they send us criminals to work the mines," he said, smiling.

"You're in a giddy mood," Marie said.

Willie smiled. "I'm just happy that I still have a job," he said, "after the stunt I pulled."

"I must say that your so-called stunt took some creativity to pull off," she said.

"I did want to become a performance artist when I was a kid," he said.

"What kind of performances?" Marie asked.

"Any kind, really," Willie said. "I'm a solid tap dancer, and I did theater and sang in a band in my youth."

"Why didn't you pursue it professionally?" Marie asked.

"My parents died when I was young, and I lived with my grandparents in the countryside," he said.

"Got myself into some trouble, out of pure boredom, I think, and went to prison for a while."

Marie's eyes widened.

"The janitorial job I got here at Zebra was my first real job when I got out," he said.

"I had no idea," Marie said.

"This was before your time," Willie said, "but Richard took a big chance on me back in the day. It helped me sort out my life and get back on the straight and narrow."

Marie just looked at him, not quite knowing what to say.

"Getting to study hardware and being promoted to a hardware engineer was a huge step up for me," Willie continued. "So, never mind about being unable to use my creativity."

"It doesn't have to stop here, though," Marie said.

"Well, I don't see much need for more sugar stunts in our corporate life," he said.

Marie laughed. "Willie, the reason I came down here was to ask about the daily scrums in the engineering teams," she said.

"You mean the ones we don't have anymore?" he said with a shrug. "The ones that are pure performance theater?"

"How do you mean?" she asked.

"I told you that the engineers are close to breaking point," he said. "Haven't you heard about the quality issues we've been having with ASLO?"

"No, what quality issues?" she asked.

"The ones that have been forcing our ratings down and filling our call center queues with customer complaints," he said.

"What's happening with ASLO?" she asked.

"We're not talking about what's happening with ASLO," Willie said. "No daily scrums mean no issues are discussed or resolved."

"How long has this been happening?" Marie asked.

"Ever since Anne left," he said. "Anne compensated for it by talking to each of us individually. She made sure that information still traveled between the different teams, even though we weren't allowed to meet up and discuss problems anymore. That's why she quit. No one person can compensate for corporate stupidity."

Marie's eyes moved from side to side. "But why aren't you allowed to meet in the first place?" she asked.

Willie smirked. "You can ask Jenni that," he said. He looked Marie in the eyes again. "And do it quick before you have a mutiny on your hands."

Mutiny

Marie didn't even bother attending the daily scrum on Tuesday morning. Instead, she scheduled a meeting with Jenni in the afternoon. Jenni was waiting for Marie in the conference room on the engineering floor.

"It's like a whiteboard grave out there," Marie remarked, pointing to the hallway.

"There was no room for them in the basement," Jenni said.

Marie smirked. "That's true," she said, "unless Shaine actually manages to clean it up."

Jenni looked sternly at Marie. "I told him to stay out of the basement," she said.

"Why?" Marie said. "At least he was making himself useful."

Jenni shook her head.

"He may actually be capable," Marie said, "but we've put him in an impossible situation."

"None of them are capable," Jenni said.

Marie raised her eyebrows. "None of them?" she repeated in surprise.

"Have you heard about the issues we're having with ASLO?" Jenni asked.

"Yes, someone mentioned that we're having issues," Marie said, "but I don't know their nature."

Jenni leaned into the table and looked from side to side. "We're seeing so many bugs," she said. Then she moved in even closer. "Our customers hate the new layout," she said, pushing her chair back.

Marie looked at her. "Jenni, these are the engineers who built ASLO," she said. "They're very capable."

"They *were* capable," Jenni said. "Now they're all slackers."

Marie clenched her jaw. "Is that why you're telling them to code, code, code?" Marie asked.

Jenni looked straight at Marie. "That's their job," she said.

"Is it," Marie said, "or is it to create a product that our customers love?"

"Same thing," Jenni said.

"Not the same thing," Marie said. "What you call coding involves more than sitting at a desk and writing code."

"Don't you HR me," Jenni said. "I've been an engineer my whole life. I've seen the likes of you telling engineers to prance around and innovate. I'm gonna let you in on a secret: code gets written by actually—gasp—writing it."

"I don't dispute that," Marie said, "or your experience and expertise in this area."

Jenni rolled her eyes.

"Remember during your interviews for this job, you said that you'd always been seen as an outsider by the male coders you worked with, and you wanted to be at a company led by a woman?" Marie asked.

"Natalie is hardly a typical woman," Jenni said. "I've never worked under a more masculine leadership style."

Marie thought for a moment. "I guess you're right," she said, "Natalie could be seen as masculine in her approach."

"Do you know how hard she pushes me to deliver results?" Jenni asked.

"I don't," Marie said, "but I do see how she pressures Mark."

"She pressures all of us," Jenni said.

Marie could swear that she saw Jenni's eyes tearing up. But when she spoke, there was no quiver in her voice.

"She's set me a target to improve quality by 15%," she said, "month to month."

"Wow, 15%," Marie said. "That seems high to me."

"That's unobtainable," Jenni said, putting her hands in her lap.

"When did she set this goal?" Marie asked.

"Shortly before Anne left," Jenni said. "Or … was fired." Jenni looked at the floor.

"Don't worry," Marie said, "Mark already told me that Anne was fired."

Jenni looked up. "She tried to rebel," Jenni said, "and Natalie wouldn't listen at all."

"Did you support her rebellion?" Marie asked.

"I was brand new," she said. "I didn't have any chips to spend with Natalie."

"But did you agree?" Marie asked.

"Yes," Jenni said, "but look where it got Anne," she added.

Marie thought for a moment. "Let me get this straight," she said. "Natalie set this new quality goal for you; Anne rebelled; you moved all the stand-ups to a virtual setting and got rid of the boards; Anne started compensating by talking to everyone individually instead; and then Anne got fired. And we've been slipping deeper and deeper into quality issues ever since."

Jenni nodded ever so slightly.

"But, Jenni," Marie said, "do you actually believe that having developers sitting at their desks and coding, coding, coding, without talking to each other about issues, is going to get us the best possible results?"

Jenni looked up at the ceiling. "Obviously not," she said. Then she looked at Marie. "And all the engineers hate me. I'm an outsider again."

Later that day, in a meeting with Mark, Marie was lost in thought.

"Marie," Mark said. "Marie," he repeated.

Marie looked up.

"Which recruitment agency do you think we can rely on for the CFO position?" Mark said, repeating his original question.

It was late afternoon, and they were in Mark's office brainstorming how to attract the right kind of CFO talent. She couldn't stop thinking about her conversation with Jenni. It was unlike any other interaction she had had with Jenni so far. Jenni usually held herself like a dock worker. Tough, assertive, and to the point. Seeing her vulnerable side made Marie question everything she had assumed about her and how to approach the looming mutiny in the engineering department. Was it within Jenni's hands to change anything at all?

Damn it, she thought. *It's a system problem, just like Anne preaches.*

"Boy, are you distracted," Mark said. "Is everything good on the home front?"

"What?" Marie asked.

"You're staring into empty space, Marie," Mark said, "just like Natalie before her divorce."

"I'm not getting a divorce," Marie said.

Mark laughed. "Now I've got your attention," he said.

"Sorry," she said, "I've just had an interesting conversation with Jenni today."

"You know what," he said, "she was here right before you came in."

"What did she want?" Marie said.

"It was interesting, indeed," Mark said. "She asked if we could lower Shaine's salary to the level of the other engineers."

Marie raised her eyebrows. "That's a radical move," she said.

"Yes," Mark said, "and I asked her to speak to Paul. It would be a great signal to the other engineers, but we need to make sure that we're on firm legal footing."

"You're actually considering it?" she said.

"It seems like he's a lot of trouble," he said, "so even if we lose him, that may not be the biggest loss. If we bring him on par with the other engineers, maybe they'll include him, and he can contribute."

Marie looked at him.

"It's a way to nudge the system toward equilibrium," he said.

Marie laughed. "Now you sound like Anne," she said.

"Well," he said, "she wasn't entirely wrong."

Marie smiled. "I think we should go with CXO Recruitment Group," she said.

Mark looked at the brochures laid out on his desk. "I tend to agree," he said.

It was Wednesday morning, and Marie met Paul in the kitchenette. They were both getting coffee.

"So, how do we tell them?" Paul asked.

"I still can't believe it's legal," Marie said, "and that you're on board with it."

"I don't like dysfunction any more than you do," Paul said, "and offering Shaine twice the salary of his peers has created a lot of dysfunction."

Marie was about to say something.

"I know that I approved it in the first place," he said.

"Why did you?" Marie asked.

"Frankly, I didn't think he would tell anyone," Paul said.

Marie looked at him. Then Paul cracked a smile. Marie began laughing and then stopped abruptly, unsure if he was serious.

"I think the question is how we tell Shaine," Marie said.

"Jenni and I already agreed," he said. "I'll meet with him. Jenni will also be there."

"He'll be upset," Marie said.

"I'm a grown man," Paul said.

Marie nodded.

"But we do need to consider how to tell the other engineers," Paul said.

"I can take care of that," Marie said.

"Good," Paul said. "We're doing it later today."

"Once you set out to do something, you sure keep momentum," Marie said.

Paul smiled, picked up his coffee, and walked out of the kitchenette. Marie fished her phone out of her pocket and called Jenni to agree on a game plan for telling the engineers.

That afternoon, the engineering department gathered in the canteen. Marie paced as she waited for Jenni to show up. Shaine came in and sat down. He smiled at the engineer next to him and settled in his seat. Then Jenni arrived, walking toward Marie.

"He seems OK," Marie said.

"He was relieved," Jenni said.

Marie looked at Jenni.

"You were right," Jenni said, "we did put him in a difficult position."

Marie nodded and gave Jenni the microphone.

"Hi, everyone," Jenni said. "We've identified pay disparities among the engineering team that I know have been a concern for many of you."

The room went silent.

"To support our values of 'Collaboration' and 'Commitment,' we have decided to even out the pay disparities," she continued. "You all know that there have been cases of extreme outliers. These individuals have accepted revised pay on par with the rest of the engineering cohort."

The entire room looked over at Shaine.

"You took a pay cut," someone shouted.

Marie noticed that it came from Ibrahim.

"Fool," someone else shouted.

"We also want to take a closer look at the current salary levels of the rest of the cohort and make adjustments to ensure coherence," Jenni said.

At every table, people were talking. Marie looked around. Shaine was the only person sitting quietly. Her stomach knotted. This was not the reaction they had been hoping for. Some of the engineers stood up.

"Collaboration and commitment," Ibrahim shouted. "How about the value of curiosity?"

"Yeah," several engineers shouted in support.

"You keep trying to sweeten the deal with soda," he continued, "and now with money."

"All we want to do is good work," Dennis shouted.

"Yeah," another couple of engineers shouted.

"Let us work," Dennis shouted.

Marie looked over at Shaine. He was looking at the floor. Willie was sitting at the same table. Everyone else was now standing.

"You can have your soda," someone shouted and slammed a bottle of soda against the table. It spilled and dripped onto the floor.

"Hey," Marie shouted. She stood in front of Jenni.

"There will be no more coding," Dennis shouted and walked toward the exit.

A couple of engineers walked behind him.

"We want freedom," Ibrahim shouted and raised his hands in the air.

"Freedom!" half of the engineers joined in.

"Freedom! Freedom! Freedom!" Ibrahim shouted again, this time supported by all.

"Now, wait a minute—" Marie tried to interject. She looked over at Jenni and grabbed the mic from Jenni's hands. "Wait a minute," Marie said, this time amplified. Even through the mic, her voice was drowned out by the chant of the crowd. Then, her voice became muffled inside her head. She felt dizzy. She could hear her heartbeat. The blood drained from her face. *Have I had lunch today?* she thought, as crouching to the floor.

"Marie?" a voice said. "Marie?" it repeated.

Marie opened her eyes. Willie was hovering over her, now in his vest. Marie felt something soft under her head. *I'm lying on his sweatshirt,* Marie realized. She looked around. She was still in the canteen. It was quiet now. About ten engineers were standing in a circle around her.

"You scared us there," Willie said.

"What happened?" Marie asked.

"Suddenly, you collapsed," Willie said.

The engineers looked down at the floor and then at each other.

"Where is Jenni?" Marie asked.

"She left," Willie said.

"I think she went to get help," another engineer said.

Marie sat up. An engineer came out of the kitchen with an apple in his hand. He gave it to Marie, who took a bite. Then Joseph emerged from the kitchen with a soda. Marie opened the can and drank a big gulp.

"I knew I should have brought you lunch to your office today," Joseph said.

"I don't usually faint," Marie said.

"You don't faint when you eat," Joseph said, putting a hand on Marie's shoulder.

She took another sip of the soda.

"We don't usually yell at our boss," an engineer said.

The others laughed.

"What's up with you?" she asked. "What's making you so angry?"

Willie sat down on the floor next to Marie. A couple of the other engineers did, too.

"I'm a great engineer," one of them said.

"Yeah, you are," another teased.

"I am," the first engineer said, "and my kids' school uses ASLO. They used to love it. Now, the teachers pull me aside to ask what's happening with us. The latest release is like a throwback to the nineties."

"My kids' school is the same," another engineer said.

"I can't stand to lend my name to the latest release," a third engineer said.

Marie looked around.

"Why don't you just change it?" she asked. "It is your code."

"One person can't change the code of an entire release," an engineer said. "We all contribute to it."

"And we have no idea what the others are doing," Ibrahim said. He stepped into the circle surrounding Marie.

Marie looked at him and furrowed her brow.

"I let my temper get the best of me," he said, "I know."

"That makes two of us," Willie said, smiling at Marie.

"It's a mutiny," Marie said.

The engineers looked around.

"Maybe it is," Ibrahim said.

"Something needs to change," Willie added.

Marie nodded. "But not like this," she said.

The engineers nodded.

"I'll drive you home," Joseph said. "Something can change tomorrow."

The Prodigal Son

Marie hadn't anticipated this message. Jason had texted her the day before, asking if they could meet. She arrived at the café early and ordered coffee and a fruit cup. Her doctor suggested that she snack more during the day to keep her blood sugar from dipping too low. She had almost finished her coffee when Jason walked past her. She got up and walked over to him. He opened his arms in greeting, and she gave him a big hug.

"How are you, Jason?" she said, holding her hands on his shoulders.

"Well," he said, "that's what we're here to talk about."

He ordered avocado toast and coffee. "It's not what I wanted," Jason said.

"Developing software for war?" Marie said.

"Don't make fun," Jason said. "I had my reasons."

"I know," Marie said, "I didn't know how impacted you are by the war."

"I'm not impacted at all," he said. "People are dying not far from here, and I'm not impacted at all. Here I am, having a lovely brunch on a Sunday when kids as young as eighteen are dying for my freedom."

They sat in silence for a couple of minutes.

"But," Jason said, "I also realized it's completely outside my control."

Marie looked at him.

"I couldn't get into the intelligence unit. I couldn't be sent to the front. Now, I can't even convince my company to donate equipment to the war efforts. It's the same as with ASLO," he said, shaking his head. "It's as if we're all closing our eyes and pretending that this has nothing to do with us."

"I think you're right," Marie said.

Jason looked at her.

"There is nothing you can do," she said. "I'm not saying that you shouldn't care," she continued, "but you do need to realize the potential impact you can have on the situation—which is not a lot."

"That's why we're here," he said.

"Do you want to come back?" Marie asked, partially as a joke.

"I've seen your new release," Jason said.

Marie smiled.

"It's totally hopeless," he said.

They both laughed.

"You've had Drue do the UX," he said. "He's great at many things, but that is not one of them."

"I don't know Drue," Marie said.

"Really?" Jason said. "He's the tall engineer with flaming red hair."

"Oh," Marie said, "then I do know Drue."

"Also, I heard you had a mutiny last week," he said.

Marie could feel the blood flowing to her face. "What have you heard?" she asked.

"You tried to even out the pay disparity," he said, "but it was too little too late."

"Who's keeping you up to date?" Marie asked.

"Willie is," Jason said, "and Tom, Dennis, Ibrahim, Lilly, and a couple of others."

"Well, Ibrahim and Dennis were the chief trouble-makers," Marie said.

"From what I hear, so was Willie," he said, "just not this time around."

"They're desperate for change," Marie said. Then she looked down at the ground.

"People think you're that change," Jason said.

Marie looked at him. To her, it didn't seem like the engineers were her biggest fans.

"Who said that?" she asked.

"The engineers," Jason said, "and I'm saying it now."

He smiled.

"I ..." Marie said. "I don't know about that."

"You've finally broken the stalemate," Jason said. "Even Anne couldn't do that."

"What stalemate is that?" Marie asked.

"Between the focus on looking busy versus actually creating value," Jason said, "and you're making people believe again."

Marie could feel her eyes tearing up. "So, you do want to come back?" she said with a half-smile.

Jason paused. "Yes," he said, "I believe in you."

Marie could feel a tear running down her cheek.

"I might not be able to influence the course of the war in Ukraine, but I can make sure that we never release something as butt-ugly as what was just launched for ASLO," he said.

Marie was sitting in her car after she and Jason said their goodbyes. She had promised to speak to Mark to ensure he was on board with Jason coming back. Her chest felt warm as if a ray of sun had taken up residence in her ribcage. She was about to turn the key in the ignition when she heard a buzzing sound from her purse. She fished out her phone and looked at it for a couple of seconds. It was Jaque, the VP of sales, calling.

"Happy Monday, Marie," Jaque thundered.

"It is, in fact, Sunday, Jaque," Marie said.

"It won't matter that it's Monday tomorrow," Jaque continued. "I hear that you're grounded until next week."

Marie frowned.

"Did Mark tell you that?" she asked.

"No, Natalie did," he said. "Sounds like you had quite the event in the canteen the other day."

Mark had sent her home as soon as she told him about what happened. She never had a chance to tell her version to anyone else.

Jaque tore her away from her train of thought. "He's underestimating you," he said.

"Who is?" Marie asked.

"Your boss," he said. "Treating you like some delicate flower and sending you home to rest up. You're the toughest broad I've ever come across."

"You felt the urge to tell me that right this instant?" she asked.

"You should know that I've noticed that about you," he said, "but that's not why I'm calling."

"What can I do for you?" she asked.

"I can't sell a damn thing these days," he said.

"You're calling HR to complain about sales?" she said.

Jaque laughed. "I know you've been talking to Jenni's folks about their teamwork and stuff," he said, "and I think it's the root of our problems. The quality of ASLO has been going downhill, and now word is starting to spread. When my guys visit our customers, they only want to talk about the bugs in the system."

"I've heard that our latest UX was appalling," she said.

"It's not just the UX," Jaque continued. "Features that were perfectly fine before are malfunctioning. It's as if the different parts of the system stopped talking to each other."

Marie smirked. "It's because the different teams working on ASLO stopped talking to each other," she said.

"Yeah, I heard about Jenni's shut-up-and-code policy," he said.

"I'm still not sure why we're having this conversation, though," Marie said.

Jaque went quiet. "Look, Marie," he said, "I can't do my job unless you do yours. I can't sell squat unless we make better software. And we can't make better software unless you fix engineering. Our interests are aligned here. I'm calling to offer my help—whatever you need to get this train back on track, you've got it."

"Jaque," she said, "can you get me back to work tomorrow?"

"I'll call Natalie right away," he said. He hung up. Marie stared at the black screen of her phone. For an executive who spent a year avoiding her, he had suddenly come to value the softer side of running a business. Marie's phone rang again. This time, it was Natalie.

"I hear you've been grounded," Natalie said without even a hello.

"Hello, Natalie," Marie said.

"Mark is really protective of you," Natalie said, "but this seems excessive."

"I'm feeling just fine," Marie said. "I want to come back to work."

"I can't see why not," Natalie said.

"Will you tell Mark?" Marie asked.

"He'll find out soon enough," Natalie said and hung up.

Marie raised an eyebrow. Was that a yes? Will he find out when Marie shows up for work tomorrow? She looked at her phone. Maybe Mark was being protective. Maybe he had a good reason to. Marie sighed and dialed Mark's number.

"Hey, Marie," he said. "Natalie just called."

"Hi, Mark," she said. "I wasn't sure if she would."

"I appreciate you trying to warn me yourself … about going to my boss to get yourself out of sick leave," he said with a pause.

"I …" she started, but nothing more came out.

"She'll take everything you've got, Marie," he said. "Of course, I want you back as soon as possible, but not if it costs you your health."

"I want to come back so we can talk about Jason," she said.

"Jason?" Mark said. "What about him?"

"He wants to come back," Marie said. "I've just had brunch with him."

"Marie, you'll be the death of me," he said.

Pedigree And Laurels

Marie was interviewing a candidate for Frank's replacement as the CFO of Zebra Apps. He was looking straight into Marie's eyes. She was looking back at him.

"How do I feel about self-organization?" he repeated.

Marie nodded.

"Are you running a kindergarten here?" he said with a grin.

Marie looked straight at him.

"You're being serious?" he said.

"Dead serious," Marie said, restraining herself from mocking him further.

"And your finance team organizes themselves according to which tasks are most pressing?" he asked, this time tasting the concept.

"That is correct," she said and looked at her watch.

After the interview, Marie knocked on Mark's door to get his attention. He looked up and gestured for her to come in.

"He's not going to work out," Marie said and sat down.

"I hadn't realized how rare a breed Frank was as a CFO," Mark said. "Not many candidates are willing to take on a finance team that's organized like a software development team."

"I never thought about how radical Frank's way of leading was," Marie said. "He never boasted about it—it just worked."

"Richard coached him from being an accountant to being a leader," Mark said. "I guess it makes sense that he would follow Richard's way of organizing."

"Have you spoken to the finance team recently?" Mark asked. "How are they holding up without Frank?"

"I've been avoiding that topic, actually," she said, "not knowing what kind of lawsuit we currently have with Frank. And Andrea."

Mark looked at Marie. "I would rather not get you involved in that," he said.

"But I can't navigate if I don't know what it is," she said.

"Marie," he said, "you're like a sponge. You absorb all the responsibility and dive into everything."

Marie looked at him.

"The only way to keep you out of something is not to wet the sponge," he said.

"Fine," she said. "Paul is handling it."

"I need you to focus on finding me a CFO candidate who can keep running our very successful finance department," he said.

Marie looked at the CV she was holding in her hand. "That guy really did check all the boxes for the position," she sighed.

"He has the right pedigree and all the laurels," Mark said.

"So, what do we look for if we can't trust pedigree and laurels?" she asked.

On Wednesday afternoon, Jason came to the office to sign his new contract. The news had traveled fast, and a small group was gathered outside the meeting room Marie had booked. Marie had to pick up Jason at reception and walk him to the guest meeting room area. When they arrived, the assembled group started cheering and clapping.

"So glad to have you back, Jason," Willie said.

"You can take over the UX," Drue said, towering over everyone else.

Ibrahim brought out a big novelty pen and handed it to Jason. "Big news deserves big props," he said.

Lilly gave Jason a hug.

"It's good to have you back," a voice said from behind the crowd.

Marie saw Natalie standing at the far end of the room. She walked over to Jason and spread out her arms. Jason reciprocated with a hug.

"I even had Celine bring in some cakes," Natalie said. Celine started opening the boxes and distributing slices.

Marie moved closer to Natalie as she withdrew from the meeting room table. "Thank you," Marie said.

"I don't know how you got him to reconsider," Natalie said, "but well done."

"I didn't really do anything," Marie said.

"It's good for morale," Natalie said. "He's the right kind of person."

"You know," Marie said, "I was just discussing with Mark what makes the right kind of person for the CFO position."

A woman eating a piece of chocolate cake turned toward Marie and Natalie.

"You know," she said, "it doesn't even have to be a finance person." Marie looked at her. "I'm Aysha," she said. "I'm the finance partner for our development organization."

"Yeah," Marie said, "I remember you from orientation a couple of months ago."

"I've never been in a finance organization like this before," Aysha said, "but everyone knows what to do. We communicate and coordinate every day at our finance board. These are some versatile finance people you've hired. A new boss might really mess things up for us."

Natalie suddenly narrowed her eyes. "So, what would a boss do for you?" she asked.

"Since we lost Frank," Aysha said, "I feel like we've lost representation in the leadership team. He used to keep us updated on priorities, and we would adjust accordingly."

"If someone else from the management team would do the same," Natalie said, "you could continue doing your good work uninterrupted."

"I think so," Aysha said.

Natalie turned to Marie. "I have an idea," she said. "Come see me as soon as possible."

It took Marie twenty minutes to get to Jason and have him sign the new contract. Marie made a deal with Celine that she would follow Jason out when the celebration started winding down so Marie could sneak up to Natalie's office to discuss her idea. Natalie's door was open.

"It's empty up here," Marie said as she walked in.

"Close the door, will you," Natalie said.

"You had an idea?" Marie said, closing the door and sitting down in one of the chairs.

"What do you think of Jaque leading the finance department?" Natalie said.

Marie raised her eyebrows. "He's not a finance person," she said.

"This is what Aysha suggested," Natalie said. "They don't need a finance person. They need someone to connect them with the leadership team."

"Jaque …" Marie said.

"Jaque's been asking for more responsibility," Natalie said, "and for opportunities to learn new areas."

"You know," Marie said, "he is the right kind of person."

"He's not the typical finance pedigree," Natalie said, "but he gives his sales team free rein, and he's even created cross-functional teams between sales and marketing."

"Is that a recent thing?" Marie asked.

"Yeah," Natalie said, "he pitched it shortly after our offsite."

"I think this could work," Marie said.

Natalie smiled.

"Will you talk to Mark about it?" Marie asked.

"I guess he'll find out sooner or later," Natalie said, opening her laptop. "Leave the door open on your way out," she said without looking up from it.

Marie walked toward the staircase. She opened the door to the stairwell and almost bumped into Mark.

"Hey," Mark said, "Natalie pinged me and said you solved the CFO conundrum."

"She did that on her own," Marie said. "She's putting Jaque in charge of finance."

Mark closed his eyes. "And why would we want Jaque to focus on anything besides sales?" Mark asked.

"Because he wouldn't get in the way of finance doing their work," Marie said.

Mark looked at her. "You think this is a good idea?" he said.

Marie nodded. "He's the right kind of person," she said, shrugging.

Mark narrowed his lips. "You know, I have a degree in finance," he said.

Marie looked at him. "I didn't know you wanted to be CFO," she said.

Mark shook his head and walked toward Natalie's office.

The Cinnamon Master

On Thursday evening, Paul texted Marie that he was making good on his promise to bake cinnamon buns. He asked her to invite more people to eat them. As Marie poured herself coffee in the canteen on Friday morning, Joseph was setting up the buffet. She walked over to him.

"Any chance you can get away for half an hour this morning?" she asked.

"It depends," he said. "Have you found someone else to stock the soda fridges?"

"Actually," she said, "we may be getting rid of them altogether."

"Even better," he said.

"Paul has baked tons of cinnamon buns for the HR breakfast," she said, "and I would love to have you there."

"Paul is quite the baker," he said. "I'm not going to pass that up."

Marie raised her eyebrows. "Does everyone know this about Paul?" she asked.

"I follow his Instagram," Joseph said, "and I've even gifted his cookbook to my friend."

Marie's jaw dropped. "He's published a cookbook?" she exclaimed.

"Yes," Joseph said, "it came out last year."

Marie went toward the staircase. Willie and Shaine emerged from the basement, large trash bags in hand.

"Wow," Marie said. "Are there dead bodies in those?"

Willie laughed. Shaine did not.

"We're cleaning up the basement," Willie said, putting his hand on Shaine's shoulder.

"It's starting to look nice down there," Shaine said.

"Could you take a break to eat some cinnamon buns?" Marie asked. "Paul baked them."

"Paul baked?" Willie said. "I'm in!"

Shaine nodded.

Marie made her way to the kitchenette on her floor. She could hear Sheila laughing several meters away. She entered the kitchenette, and her jaw dropped. Paul was wearing an apron and handing out paper plates. Marie walked toward him. He furrowed his eyebrows. She gave him a big hug. He stood stiffly for a while, then put his arms around her, too.

"You …" she started.

"I bake," he said.

She let go of him and took a step back. "You don't just bake," she said. "You're a professional baker! And author!"

"I told you I'm the one who bakes at my house," he said, smiling.

Marie looked around.

"Only trouble is," he said, "once I start my industrial mixer, I might as well bake up a big batch."

Sheila was already eating buns and chatting to Eric. Jo was picking out a bun. Mark was pouring himself a cup of coffee. Esther walked through the door and raised her eyebrows.

"Whoa," she said, "is HR breakfast usually like this?"

"It really is not," Marie said. "This is all Paul."

Paul gave Esther a paper plate.

"Paul, I'm gonna pop by finance and gather some more mouths for all of these," Marie said.

Paul nodded.

When Marie returned with Aysha from finance and a couple of her finance colleagues, Shaine and Willie had also arrived. They had met Ibrahim and Dennis in the parking lot and invited them. Lilly from engineering was eating a bun already. Marie wasn't sure how she had gotten the message. In the corner, she also saw Natalie and Celine. While Marie was looking around, Jaque arrived.

"So, this is where all our budget goes," he thundered.

"This is all on me," Paul said.

"Don't mind if I help myself then," Jaque said.

Marie took a cinnamon bun and sat down next to Eric and Sheila. "I didn't anticipate this turning into a bakery," Marie said.

"I liked it small," Sheila said.

"Did you know about Paul's cookbook?" Marie asked.

Sheila nodded. "I gave it to my mom for Christmas," she said.

"It's really great," Eric said. "Very easy to follow. And funny."

"What else don't I know about Paul?" Marie said.

Marie saw Jo get up and drop her plate on the table. It made a light thump.

"You did what?" Jo shouted.

"We cleared the basement," Willie said.

"Where did you put it all?" Jo demanded.

"In the bins," Shaine said, "where it belongs."

Jo stormed out the door. Marie shrugged at Eric and Sheila. She noticed Ibrahim laughing next to Shaine.

"No, man, you're full of it," she heard Ibrahim say.

"I'm just saying that I was a scrum master at my former company," Shaine said, "and I think that going back to the physical boards could really help us discuss more openly."

"We've never needed scrum masters before," Willie said.

"Well, you clearly do now," Shaine said. "It's just like at my former company before their culture program."

"You think you can just change how we've done things because you took a pay cut?" Ibrahim said.

Paul also looked over at Ibrahim. Ibrahim noticed that people were looking at him now. He stood up. "We don't need an additional role," he said, "we need to talk to each other."

Shaine stood up, too. "I agree," he said. "I think my talking about my salary actually opened up some important conversations."

Marie couldn't help but laugh. Everyone looked over at her. Shaine looked hurt.

Now, it was Marie's turn to stand up. "I'm sorry," she said. "You're right. That's what's funny. It actually did lead to some great conversations." She walked over to Shaine. "I think you're right about the lack of scrum masters," she said.

"I don't need anyone telling me how to talk to people," Ibrahim said.

Jenni shouted from across the room. "What do you need then to start talking to the other teams about our bugs?" she said.

Ibrahim sat down and said, "Paul here is the cinnamon master. I'm serious. We're talking about our problems right now—without having to open Jira."

"If it will fix our bugs, I'm happy to hire Paul to bake buns every morning," Jaque said.

"Spending our money already," Natalie said. "You haven't even looked at our books yet."

Mark looked sternly at Natalie.

"Come on, Mark," Natalie said, "We're announcing that Jaque is the new CFO later this afternoon anyway."

Aysha gasped. Now, Paul looked sternly at Natalie.

Marie walked over to Jaque and shook his hand. "Congrats, Jaque," she said, "I think you will be great at the role."

Jenni congratulated him next. Aysha left the room. People soon started to disperse with cinnamon buns for their colleagues in hand. Marie sat down to eat her bun. She wanted to take a bite, but it was as if her stomach could not handle even a crumb.

"Marie," Joseph said gently, sitting down next to her, "we need to talk about your eating."

"What?" Marie said.

"When did you last eat?" he asked.

Marie thought back. She didn't manage to have breakfast that day.

"That's why you can't eat," he said. "Because you've stopped eating."

"I haven't stopped eating," Marie said.

"When your surroundings feel out of control, you control what you can. You control your food," he said.

"I forget to eat," she said.

"It starts with you forgetting to eat," he said, "but then you stop eating." Joseph looked at her and was about to say more, but Jo entered the room.

"They took it all," she said. She sat down next to Marie. "They threw it all out," Jo said. "The basement, there's nothing down there. They've even vacuumed."

"That I must see," Marie said. She looked at Joseph. "Do you want to join us in the basement?" she asked.

"I'll need to go back to the kitchen," he said.

Marie looked at Jo. "Let's get Eric and Sheila, too," she said.

The basement was empty. No server casings. No boxes. No old office chairs.

"It's so big," Sheila said.

Jo sat down on the bottom stair. She put her face in her palms. Marie sat next to her.

"This was my space," Jo said through her fingers. "This is where I would come to think and get inspired."

Marie looked at Eric and raised an eyebrow.

"Now it's all empty and corporate," Jo said.

"It's a new beginning, Jo," Sheila said.

"I liked it how it was," Jo said.

Sheila sat next to Jo and hugged her. "We'll find you some other chaos to think in," Sheila said, "like Marie's office."

"My office is neat," Marie said.

"Not after we're done with it," Sheila said. "Come on, Jo."

Jo and Sheila got up and walked up the stairs. Eric sat down next to Marie.

"Joseph is concerned about my eating," Marie said.

Eric looked at her. "Take this in the kindest way possible," he said, "but I think you're in over your head."

Marie could feel a sting in her heart.

"You know that I love you," he said, "and I would follow you to any company you worked at. But too many different aspects of Zebra are broken, and you're trying to fix them all at once."

"That's my job," she said.

"But it's more than your job," he said.

"What are you suggesting?" she asked.

Eric sighed. "I think you should join engineering for a while," he said.

"As what?" she asked.

"As a coach," he said.

Marie looked at him.

"Look, I'll look out for Sheila and Jo for a couple of months, and you can immerse yourself in helping engineering develop a different culture," he said.

"You want my job?" Marie asked.

"I can do your job," Eric said, "but I can't coach engineering to change their culture."

Marie looked at him.

"They trust you. They believe in you. It has to be you," Eric said.

Marie was about to object, but Willie and Shaine came down to the basement, and Eric and Marie congratulated them for cleaning up the mess.

Who Are We?

Marie picked Jason up at reception on Monday morning. The receptionist had just given him a big bunch of flowers when Marie hugged him.

"I don't remember the flowers being so big last time I joined," Jason said, the flowers towering over his head.

The receptionist beamed. Marie led Jason to the engineering hallway.

"I'm happy to have you back too, you know," Marie said.

"I know," Jason said, smiling.

"Now we can start fixing things," Marie said.

"Will you join us?" Jason asked.

"What do you mean?" Marie asked.

"It's not going to be enough to try and impact the organization," Jason said. "You need to be in the work."

Marie looked from side to side. "I am in the work," she said.

"You're trying to impact the work," Jason said, looking at her.

"Where is this coming from?" Marie asked.

"I heard you were asking why we don't have any scrum masters," he said.

"Who are you talking to?" Marie said. "You've just started back."

"There are many of us who care about Zebra," he said, "and about ASLO. We don't want the company to throw our work down the drain."

Marie looked him straight in the eyes.

"Not again, anyways," he said.

"That almost sounds like a threat," she said, "as if you were some group like Anonymous."

Jason smiled.

"We are the many," he said, "we are one."

"Are you joking?" Marie said and raised her eyebrows.

Jason shook his head. "We're not anonymous," he said. "You know us." He leaned in and almost whispered in Marie's ear, "We need you to teach the teams how to work together again."

Then Jason spotted Ibrahim walking down the hallway. "Ibra!" he shouted.

"You!" Ibrahim shouted. "Get in there and fix the UX!" Ibrahim patted Jason on the back and led him into the office.

Marie was left standing in the hallway, still trying to figure out who "we" were and what exactly they wanted her to do. Marie's brooding was interrupted by Jenni as she walked past her.

"You're going to be late for the meeting," Jenni said without stopping.

"What meeting?" Marie shouted after her.

"Maybe you're not in the meeting," Jenni muttered, then shouted. "Probably Mark is."

Marie followed Jenni, trying to keep up. "What meeting?" Marie shouted.

"Never mind," Jenni said and rushed off.

Mark was heading out of his office when Marie walked down the hallway toward his office. He was wearing a dark gray suit and a blue tie.

"Mark," she shouted.

"I really need to be upstairs," Mark said.

"What's happening upstairs?" she asked.

"I'll have to tell you later," he said. He took a deep breath and headed toward the staircase.

What the—? thought Marie. She went into her office and opened her laptop. She opened Mark's calendar. It was blocked out until 1 p.m. with an invite marked "Private." She opened Natalie's calendar. The same duration was blocked. She opened Jenni's and Jaque's. Same block. Finally, she opened Natalie's assistant Celine's calendar. Her calendar had the same block, but earlier that morning, she had an entry titled "Remember croissants for buyer meeting."

Buyers, Marie thought. *Buyers of what?*

She felt a deep pit open in her stomach. What was Natalie selling? Marie couldn't help herself. She got up from her chair and walked up to Natalie's floor.

She opened the door from the stairwell to the floor as quietly as she could and tiptoed inside. Laughter was coming from the board meeting room next to Natalie's office. She saw Mark shaking hands with a tall man with a white beard.

Where have I seen that man before? Marie thought. Then she locked eyes with Jaque. He looked sternly at her and slowly shook his head from side to side. She closed the door and scurried down, her heart pounding.

Marie was pacing back and forth in her office when Eric walked in.

"You're going to wear a hole in the carpet," Eric said.

Marie smirked. "This has been a weird morning," she said.

"What's weird about it?" Eric asked.

"Jason was talking about a grander 'we' that seems to want me to get 'in' the work," Marie said, "and Mark is up there meeting with someone whom Celine has labeled 'buyers' in her calendar."

Eric nodded, closed the door behind him and sat down in the armchair.

"We might be getting sold then," he said.

Marie stopped pacing and looked at him. She sat at the edge of her desk. "We might," she said.

"Do you think Jason was talking about the buyers?" Eric asked.

"For a moment, I thought he was talking about you and your suggestion that I coach engineering," Marie said.

"What exactly did he say?" he asked.

"He asked about what I'd said about the lack of scrum masters," she said, "and said that I need to join the engineering team."

"I tend to agree," Eric said. "I didn't speak to him, Marie," he continued. "We never had that kind of relationship. We're not really on the same wavelength like the two of you. We might just be looking at the situation and drawing the same conclusions."

"What wavelength would that be?" Marie asked.

"You get him, Marie," Eric said. "I struggle with developing that sort of rapport with our engineers."

"Who do you get?" Marie asked.

Eric sighed. "I get you."

Marie sat down in her office chair and folded her hands. "What exactly are you proposing?" she asked.

Eric looked down and shook his head. "Look," he said, finally looking up. "I'd suggest that you take on the task of coaching the engineering teams through our current challenges. We're all in trouble if ASLO continues its downward spiral. There will be no HR department to lead if we don't fix our quality issues, and to fix our quality issues, we need to fix our engineering teams."

Marie sighed.

"The engineers trust you," he said. "They believe you can be that change."

"Anne was that change," Marie said, "and look where it got her."

Eric shook his head. "Anne wasn't change," he said. "Anne never had Natalie's ear like you do. To achieve change, you need actual power."

"You think I have power?" Marie said, raising her eyebrows.

Eric smiled. "You're the most powerful person in our company," Eric said.

Marie blushed.

"I don't mean you're a power-hoarder," Eric said. "I just mean that you've managed to get influence with both our senior leadership and employees. You're a hero to both sides of the divide."

"And what about you?" she asked. "Do you crave power?"

Eric's eyes teared up. "That's not what this is about," he said.

"But you want to lead HR development while I take an unnamed role in engineering?" she said.

Eric looked away. "It hurts that you perceive it that way," he said.

"How should I perceive it?" she asked.

"It's all about comparative advantages," he said. "I can lead Sheila and Jo through our team's assignments. I've done it before. You can do that, too, or you can choose to wield your power to transform the biggest constraint on our company's survival."

"And what happens after our company survives?" Marie asked.

"*If* it survives," Eric said, pointing at the ceiling. He then looked at Marie. "I'm surprised that it matters so much to you to be head of HR development," he said.

"Of course it means a lot to me," Marie said, "I've worked hard to achieve this position."

"I don't doubt it," Eric said, "but your power doesn't come from your job title."

"The title helps," Marie said.

"The title only gets you in the room," he said. "It doesn't earn you the power to stay in it—to maneuver the course of events."

Marie shook her head.

"Look, Marie," he said, "I was head of HR development at Sailtech, where Mark and I worked together. I did everything to the best of my ability when it came to coaching, training, and developing our people. You know I can do this well. But I didn't even have a tenth of the power you have at Zebra."

"Sailtech was a bigger company," Marie said.

"That's not it," he said. "Power is personal. Being competent isn't enough." He sighed again. "I wish I could have done what you've done here; then, I might have had a different career trajectory. At my age, I could have been VP of HR somewhere. But that's not something I can master. I support the powerful person. I'm the person behind the person, and I accept and cherish that role."

Marie suddenly felt a needling sensation in her heart. "You want to be VP of HR?" she asked.

"It's the same as asking me if I want a million dollars," he said. "It would be nice, but it's not going to happen."

"I thought you liked your role?" she said.

"I love my role," he said, "and I love being the person behind you. I've embraced what I can and can't do and take pride in serving you. But, if you ask me if I wish I was different, then yes—yes, I do. I wish I was more like you."

"You're the one who keeps our team together," she said.

"I don't refute that I play an important role," he said, "but having a well-functioning team isn't enough if you can't ensure it's anchored to leadership. I'll look after Jo and Sheila and keep the ship afloat. We have enough goodwill that your focusing on something else for a few months won't endanger our position in the company."

Marie got up from her chair and walked toward the window. "Is that what engineering needs?" she asked. "Anchoring to leadership?"

"Jenni doesn't speak up for their cause," Eric said. "She just pays lip service to Natalie. And she doesn't know anything about building products."

"I don't know anything about building products," Marie said.

"No, but you're smart enough to listen to those who do," Eric said.

Hooded Men-Children

Sheila and Jo transformed Marie's office. They installed a long bar table in the middle of the room. They lined the walls with bookshelves stocked with different kinds of paper, markers, googly eyes and hot glue guns. Marie, Jo, Sheila, and Eric poured champagne at the room's unveiling on Thursday afternoon.

"It's almost as good as the basement," Jo said.

"Almost?" Sheila asked. "Girl, this is the deluxe version of your basement."

Paul and Esther entered the room. Paul was holding a box.

"My daughter would love this room," Esther said, looking around.

"Your daughter is five," Paul said.

Sheila and Jo laughed.

"Don't judge our process," Sheila said. "I don't judge your big-ass spreadsheets."

Esther put her hand on Sheila's shoulder. "My spreadsheets are spotless," she said. They both laughed.

"What's in the box, Paul?" Marie asked.

"A cake," Paul said. "I wasn't sure how to frame this occasion exactly. Is it a promotion? Demotion? A kind of leave of absence?"

Marie smiled. He opened the box and revealed a bright yellow cake with the words "Go save ASLO" on it.

"I think you got the occasion just right, Paul," she said.

Marie was walking down the stairs with a box of her stuff when she met Natalie walking up. Natalie looked at Marie's box.

"When you commit to something, you commit," Natalie said.

"What do you mean?" Marie said.

"I mean, when I asked you to fix our culture," Natalie said, "I meant hire a consultant who can do some pretty slides for us, not leave your executive role and move in with our engineers."

"They are our culture," Marie said.

"Shouldn't Jenni be fixing engineering?" Natalie said. "You know, my head of engineering?"

"Jenni asked me to work my HR magic," Marie said.

Natalie shrugged. "That Eric of yours isn't going to cut it as your replacement," she said, "he's too weak."

"He'll manage for a couple of months," Marie said.

Natalie was about to walk past, but Marie interrupted her. "Who was that gentleman with the white beard in the conference room with all of you the other day?"

Natalie turned around. "Nothing gets past you," she said, her eyes sparkling. She stepped down to the same level as Marie. "That's why I can't have you hanging out in the basement with a bunch of hooded men-children."

"Who was he?" Marie repeated. "I think I've seen him before."

Natalie smiled, turned on her heel, and started walking up the stairs again.

"Natalie?" Marie called after her.

Natalie turned around.

"He's the CTO of ConvoSystems," Natalie said and winked.

I've never met the CTO of ConvoSystems, Marie thought. Suddenly, it struck her—*Richard is the new CTO of ConvoSystems.* Richard, who cofounded Zebra Apps with Natalie.

Jason greeted Marie when she reached their new shared office, where she would sit across from Drue.

"Is it true," he asked, "that Richard was here?"

Marie swallowed. "Richard who?" she asked.

"Come on, Marie," Jason said, "you must have seen him."

"Who's Richard?" Shaine asked.

"The founder of Zebra," Jason said.

"I thought Natalie was the founder of Zebra?" Shaine said.

"She's half of the founding team," Marie clarified. "She and Richard founded it together."

"He's at your former employer now," Jason said.

"Good for him," Shaine said.

"Dude!" Drue exclaimed.

"I mean, it's great that he's found another job," Shaine said.

"You are seriously clueless, man," Jason said.

"What do you want me to say?" Shaine said.

"Richard is the new CTO of ConvoSystems," Drue said, "and he has a meeting with Natalie now that Zebra is in trouble. Do the math, dude."

"Like you did the math for the UX of ASLO?" Shaine said.

Drue stood up, towering over the remaining three. "Unwarranted, man," he said. "I've never done UX before in my life."

"How did you end up doing the UX for that release?" Jason asked.

"They were just lying there in Jira," Drue said, "the stories related to UX. I had finished all my other stories, and we were running behind. I couldn't just let them sit there."

"Very noble of you," Shaine said, "but maybe you should have left them there."

Drue sat down. "That's hurtful, man."

"I think you did the right thing," Marie said.

Drue looked up.

"If we don't have anyone with the skill set to solve the task," she said, "all we can do is try our best."

"You could have asked for help," Shaine said.

"I did," he said, nodding toward Jason.

"You asked too late, my friend," Jason said.

"I meant me," Shaine said, putting his arms at his sides.

"I didn't know you have front-end experience," Jason said.

"No one here knows anything about what I can do," Shaine replied.

"We know you're willing to get paid handsomely for it," Drue said.

"Now, Drue," Marie said, "that's a settled matter."

Shaine was looking down at his desk. "How was I supposed to know what the rest of you were earning?" he said.

Drue and Jason started working on their computers.

Marie pushed her chair next to Shaine's desk. He looked up from his computer. "So what can you do, Shaine?" she asked.

Mastering Scrum

Marie had spent the past few weeks interviewing the engineers about what they preferred doing, what skills they brought to the table, and which parts of ASLO they had worked on. She put all her notes up on one of the vacant whiteboards in the hallway. It looked like the pinboard of a murder case detective, with thread going from one person to the next, indicating who worked on the different elements of ASLO. In the corner was a cluster of names of everyone who had worked as scrum masters at their former companies. Marie had invited those team members to huddle at the board.

"It looks like spaghetti," Lilly said.

"It accurately represents our architecture," Tom said.

"You all have experience working as scrum masters at your former companies," Marie said, "and I have a hypothesis that we need to introduce scrum masters in our development teams to stop the spaghetti."

"I don't know if scrum masters are what we need," Shaine said.

Marie looked at him. "You literally suggested that we need scrum masters two weeks ago," she said.

"I think we need to fix our architecture first," he replied.

"You feel that fixing our architecture is more important than fixing the collaboration of our teams?" she asked.

"Yes," he said, "our teams are just confused about what they should be doing."

Marie looked at him.

"I disagree," Lilly said. "Our architecture is a mess because our teams are a mess."

"That's how it is," Tom said. "Architecture follows organizational structure."

"How did you deal with this at your previous companies?" Marie asked.

"We had a firm governance process," Shaine said. "No one could make any changes without the architecture board's approval."

"We tried different things," Lilly said. "We tried having platform-oriented teams and functional value stream teams. Most important was not which teams we had, but how these teams worked."

"Yeah," Tom said, "we also tried different team structures, but we mainly realized that making sure people speak to each other and feel ownership for resolving issues was most important."

"How are you organized now?" Marie asked.

Tom and Lilly looked at each other.

"We're organized per customer," Lilly said.

"That means when we get a new customer for ASLO," Tom said, "Jenni assigns a team that will work on customizing the platform to fit their needs."

"So, many different teams are changing what ASLO does at the same time?" Marie asked.

"Yes," Lilly said, "and right now, those teams aren't talking to each other."

Marie could feel the blood flowing to her face. "That's not what the organizational chart shows," she said.

"No," Shaine said, "officially, we're organized according to features."

"Jenni appoints people from each feature team to each client, and they essentially focus on that client and not the features," Lilly said.

"Wait," Marie said, "so people are in two teams?"

"Now the feature teams don't really have anything in common," Tom said. "The customer teams are the primary unit."

"But how do we resolve differences between different customers and their needs when they impact the same part of the system?" Marie asked.

"We don't," Tom said.

Shaine pulled out his fist and made an explosion with his hand.

There were only a couple of cars left in the parking lot. Marie had been sitting and looking out at the lot since it had been full of cars. *How could this be?* she thought. *We've built a successful product that was really needed—that was important—and now we've made a mess out of it.* She looked at her phone. *Should I call her?* she thought. She dialed Anne.

"When did it begin?" Marie asked.

"Marie?" Anne said.

"Yes," Marie said. "When did the decay begin?"

Anne was quiet. "Where are you, Marie?" Anne asked.

"In the parking lot at Zebra," Marie said.

"Let's meet at the coffee shop," Anne suggested.

Marie parked behind the coffee shop and walked inside. Anne was already sitting in the corner that faced both sides of the street. Marie walked toward the table.

"You asked when it all began," Anne said.

Marie nodded.

"What have you uncovered?" Anne asked.

Marie suddenly felt uneasy. Was Anne just trying to get information? Who would she share this information with? Marie looked toward the door. To her surprise, Jaque walked in. She locked eyes with him, and he waved at her.

"Did you know that Jaque would be coming?" Marie asked.

Anne shook her head. Jaque walked toward them.

"I was looking for you all afternoon," he said, looking at Marie. He shrugged and sat down. He took Marie's plate and took a bite of her cinnamon bun. "You never eat these things anyway," Jaque said.

Marie rolled her eyes. Jaque took a sip of her tea.

"Hey," Marie said, "I'd already taken a sip of that."

Jaque shrugged. "We're all one big sharing family now," he said, "or at least we're going to be."

Marie slammed the palm of her hand down on the table. "Enough!" she said. It was, indeed, enough to get the whole coffee shop to turn their heads toward Marie. Marie blushed, slouched back, and spoke softly, "You're both going to tell me what's going on, right now!"

Jaque took another sip of Marie's tea and angled his chair toward her. "Marie," he said, "I was looking for you because I needed someone to talk to about the current financial situation at Zebra Apps. I need someone with a cool head to help me make sense of it." He smiled. "I'm not so sure you're the cool-headed person I thought you were."

Marie gently hit him on his shoulder.

"Aw," he said, rubbing his shoulder, "you're spending way too much time with our engineers. You're turning into a dude."

"Why are you spending time with the engineers?" Anne asked.

"ASLO is broken because our teams are broken," Marie said, "so I've moved in with the engineers to help mend our team culture."

"You're going in the work," Anne said.

"Have you been talking to Jason?" Marie said.

"We're not anonymous," Anne continued. "You know who we are."

"You and Jason, I've figured out," Marie said. "Who else is there?"

"I am one," Jaque said, raising his hand.

Marie raised her eyebrows. "You're in cahoots with Anne and Jason?" she asked.

"Is that so hard to believe?" Jaque said. "I also want Zebra to survive."

Marie threw her hands up in the air. "Is Natalie part of this rescue effort?" she said.

Jaque looked from one side to the other before pulling his chair closer to the table and leaning in. "Even though Natalie has been chasing impossible sales targets, keeping all our expenses under control, and not investing in any new products," he paused, "we've never been less profitable. I've been going through the numbers with our accountants, who are very open and transparent, I must say."

Marie looked at him.

"Oh, I'm losing my train of thought," Jaque said, "but they really are a pleasure to work with. They've been trying to get Natalie's attention for the past year, but she won't listen."

"I know how that feels," Anne said.

"What are they trying to get her attention about?" Marie asked.

"That we're leaking money," Jaque said. "We may not be able to survive until the end of the year."

Marie opened her mouth in disbelief. "But ASLO is used across most schools in the region. We've just entered Germany and have a hard time keeping up with our orders there."

"That is all true," Anne said, "but we charge a flat installation fee and a yearly subscription fee per institution. Most of the cost of new development isn't covered by that."

Jaque raised a finger in the air. "Exactly," he said, "our business model is optimized to get money now—not to build a sustainable company."

"Marie," Anne said, "it's not just the teams struggling."

"Natalie is struggling too," Jaque said.

"Is that why Richard was at that buyer's meeting?" Marie asked. "Is ConvoSystems going to buy us?"

"I asked Richard to take that meeting," Jaque said.

"I would have bet my money on Anne," Marie said.

"I didn't know the state of Zebra's finances," Anne said.

"But how would ConvoSystems benefit from purchasing Zebra?" Marie asked. "We aren't even in the same industry."

"That's why it's a hard thing to make happen," Jaque said, "and why we need your help."

"The alternatives are worse," Anne said.

"What are the alternatives?" Marie asked. "Closing Zebra Apps?"

“Why do you think we didn’t offer ASLO to children fleeing the war in Ukraine?” Jaque asked.

Marie’s eyes widened.

“There are buyers that could be worse than a bad product match,” Anne said.

“Who did Natalie try to sell to?” Marie exclaimed.

“I don’t know for sure,” Anne said. “I don’t have any proof.”

“I do,” Jaque said. “I’ve gone through Natalie’s expenses from last year. There are several trips to Russia.”

“That’s not proof,” Anne said.

“That can’t be right …” Marie faltered. “She wouldn’t. How could she even enter Russia?”

“To be fair,” Jaque said, “we clearly didn’t make a deal.”

“So, perhaps Natalie had a change of heart and didn’t go through with it,” Anne said.

“Or the deal fell through,” Jaque said.

“Who is Natalie,” Marie said, “and what matters to her?”

The Day After

Marie did not feel like getting out of bed that Saturday. The conversation with Jaque and Anne kept replaying in her head. Thomas popped his head into the bedroom. He had been watching cartoons with Ally in the living room while Marie lay in the bedroom in the dark.

"Would you mind Ally watching cartoons up here with you for a while?" he asked. "I really want to go for a run."

Ally walked in, holding her iPad and wearing her kitty ear headphones.

"Come here, sweetie," Marie said as Ally climbed into bed with her. Marie kissed her daughter's cheeks and snuggled into her. She stroked her hair and her fluffy pajamas. "What are you watching, baby?" she asked. When there was no reply, Marie took off one of Ally's earphones. "What are you watching?" she repeated.

"It's about an elephant who wants to be a bird because he's friends with birds. He's unhappy because he can't fly. Then, one day, the birds' tree falls down, and the elephant can put it back up because he is strong," Ally said.

"So, he understands that it's good to be an elephant," Marie says.

Ally nodded and put her hand over Marie's. Marie smiled and started to doze off. Then, a thought struck her: *What kind of animal would Zebra Apps be? What was it inherently good at? Were they trying to be a different animal altogether? Is that why they were sad?*

She got up to get a pad of paper.

Is It A Zebra?

Lilly, Tom, and Jo greeted Marie in the conference room on the engineering floor. The room was plastered with brown paper. On the whiteboard, Marie replicated the drawing she had made on Saturday based on Ally's cartoon.

"Is she coming?" Tom asked.

"I don't think she'll like this," Lilly said.

"She's the head of engineering," Marie said. "Ultimately, it's her decision how we're organized."

"I like that you say 'we,'" Tom said.

"What is all this?" Jenni asked, looking around the room.

"We've traced the quality problems we have with ASLO to how we're organized," Lilly said, "and we would like to take you through our thinking."

Jenni looked Lilly up and down. Lilly kept her gaze firmly locked on Jenni.

"You're never one to hold back your opinions, Lilly," Jenni said.

Marie raised her eyebrows and looked at Jo. Jo shrugged.

"Jenni," Marie started, "would you prefer we take you through this in a smaller group?"

Jenni showed her teeth.

Marie looked around at Lilly, Tom, and Jo. "Would you please excuse us?" Marie said to them.

"But …" Jo started and then stopped when Marie slowly shook her head.

"Let us know if you need anything," Tom said.

They left the room. Jenni's shoulders dropped.

"What was that about?" Marie asked.

"What?" Jenni asked.

"You're not a fan of Lilly?" Marie said.

"Goddam know-it-all," Jenni said.

"Anything you want to talk about?" Marie said.

Jenni looked at Marie. "Why am I looking at an elephant?" Jenni asked, pointing to the wall.

Marie laughed. "Inspiration strikes in weird places sometimes," she said. She walked over to the whiteboard. "ASLO is like an elephant—or whatever animal; it doesn't matter which. If we try to fight what we are, we'll never succeed. The purpose of this exercise is to define what kind of animal ASLO is and decide how we organize ourselves to make sure we actually align with our animal spirit."

"That is serious HR mumbo jumbo, Marie," Jenni said and smiled.

"Wouldn't we be a zebra," Jenni said, "if ASLO was an animal?"

"Somehow, I didn't think of that," Marie said. "That would have been a more obvious choice."

"Zebra it is, then," Jenni said.

Marie nodded.

"Take me through your mumbo jumbo," Jenni said.

Marie walked over to the brown paper tacked to the wall and drew a circle. "These are our customers," Marie said. "Mainly schools and other educational institutions."

Jenni nodded.

"They pay a flat fee for subscribing to the platform, and they can use it for as many students as they wish," Marie said.

"Yes," Jenni said, "Natalie's vision was to make sure we're in every classroom all over the country—and now also in every classroom in Germany."

"We are, in fact, in most classrooms already," Marie said. "So much so that our engineers are cornered by unhappy parents and teachers when they go about their day. But, for every instance of ASLO, we make considerable adjustments to the platform," Marie said, drawing another circle. "To do so, we create a new team for each new customer."

"Yes," Jenni said, "those are our delivery teams. They make sure that the customer is happy with their system. They keep in touch with their customer daily and continue adjusting the platform even after the initial implementation period."

"Exactly," Marie said. She drew smaller circles inside the delivery team circle. "In the delivery team, we have individual developers," she said, "and these developers technically belong to feature teams." She drew a bigger circle next to the delivery team. "This is our platform," she said. She drew circles inside the platform circle, followed by lines between the team members in the delivery team circle and the smaller circles in the platform teams.

"Yes," Jenni said, "that's how we make sure that the changes for each client are aligned across the entire platform."

"But what defines these feature teams?" Marie asked.

"They have common backlogs," Jenni said.

"Does anyone maintain those backlogs?" Marie said.

Jenni was about to object.

"I don't want to put you on the spot," Marie said. "We investigated this. The feature team backlogs aren't maintained. The feature teams don't sit together—people sit in their delivery teams. The stand-ups for the feature teams are non-existent. *De facto,* those teams do not exist."

Jenni looked at the circles Marie had drawn.

"So, even though we have a mechanism for adjudicating changes to the platform, in reality, it doesn't happen," Marie said. She sat down at the table next to Jenni.

"So that is why ASLO is breaking," Jenni said, still looking ahead.

"I think so," Marie said, looking at Jenni. "It's also an issue that we don't actually fund the feature teams. We only fund delivery—not the continuous improvement we need to maintain a solid platform." Marie said.

"That is Jaque's department," Jenni said.

Marie smiled. "I think you and I should talk to Jaque," Marie said.

Peanut-Shaped

Marie was pouring herself a cup of coffee in the kitchenette on the engineering floor. She had briefed Tom, Lilly, and Jo on her progress with Jenni. They were in disbelief that Jenni had listened.

Willie entered the kitchenette. "What's going on in the conference room?" he asked, pointing toward the glass wall plastered with brown paper.

"We're discussing how the current quality issues with ASLO may be rooted in how we're organized and how we fund the development of ASLO," Marie said.

"You know, when we talk about funding, we should also remember to fund the hardware in the data center when we make changes to ASLO," he said.

"How do you mean?" Marie asked.

"Have a seat," Willie said and gestured toward the table.

Marie sat down.

"Whatever we build with software actually runs on our hardware," he said, pointing in the direction of the data center. "Lately, ASLO has been occupying more and more physical space and requiring more power to run. It means we keep adding computing power and storage to the data center. Because of the war and the aftermath of the pandemic, it's very hard to get the parts needed to expand the data center."

"How do we cope?" Marie asked.

"We pay more for the spare parts we can find," Willie said, "but we've also looked into buying used hardware from data centers that are being closed down."

"Who would close down their data centers?" Marie asked.

Willie looked at her. "The large Western companies tried to get out of the Russian market when the war started," Willie said, "and there were spare parts to be swept up cheaply for a short time."

Marie gasped. "Did we buy spare parts from Russia?" she asked. Willie nodded. Marie's jaw dropped. Those expenses that Jaque had found. "Did Natalie go to Russia?" she asked.

"I believe so," Willie said, "and so did Frank and Andrea."

"Who else knows about this?" Marie asked.

Willie shrugged. "I don't think anyone was particularly proud of that move," Willie said, "and it was short-lived anyway. We only managed to get one shipment before Russia shut down completely."

Suddenly, a thought struck Marie. "Wait, so Frank and Andrea were on the same trip to Russia?" Marie said.

"I believe so," Willie said.

Marie got up to leave.

"Wait, Marie," Willie said. "I'm serious. When you talk about the cost of ASLO, remember the cost of increasing the data center every time we build new features or add new customers."

Marie was on her way to Paul's office to discuss what she had learned about Frank and Andrea traveling together when she ran into Jaque on the stairs.

"Marie," Jaque said, "aren't we meeting now?"

Marie stopped. "Right," she said, turning around, "we are."

Jaque smirked. "What's going on?" he asked.

"Natalie was, in fact, in Russia," she said, "with Frank and Andrea to purchase used elements for our data center."

Jaque raised his eyebrows. "I see," he said.

"We only got one batch of hardware, though," she said.

"So it wasn't to sell the company to the Russians," Jaque said.

Marie thought for a minute. "We don't know that for sure," she said.

"It wasn't discussed with me or Jenni," he said. "You seem flustered, Marie."

"I'm just confused," Marie said. "I'm not sure what to do with this new information."

"Right now, nothing," Jaque said. "Let's go talk to Jenni." He grabbed Marie's shoulders and led her to the meeting room.

Jenni was already there. Marie walked over to her drawing of circles.

"There's a circle missing," Marie said. She drew one more circle before the platform and wrote "data center" in the middle. "Every time we create new features for ASLO, we also increase our physical footprint in the data center."

"What am I looking at?" Jaque said. "Peas?"

"You're looking at how engineering is organized and funded," Jenni said.

"We've identified why we have failing quality," Marie said.

Jenni walked up to the wall and explained the circles.

"Also, we don't fund the increases in the data center as we add new features," Marie said.

"So, that's why we're bleeding money," Jaque said, "because we only charge for one-third of the work we actually deliver."

Marie nodded.

"That's why we need you to charge for our products in a way that allows us to fund all the steps in our development," Jenni said to Jaque.

"Why do we have a data center at all?" Jaque asked.

Jenni raised her eyebrows.

"I'm not kidding," Jaque said. "If it's a third of our costs, we don't currently fund it, and we have a hard time finding the parts we need for it—what if we sell off the parts we have?"

"And migrate to the cloud," Jenni said quietly.

"We could make a profit in the short term," Jaque continued, "helping Zebra survive here and now as we rework our cost structure."

Jaque walked over to the brown paper. He drew a line around the delivery team and the platform.

"We can go from pea-shaped to peanut-shaped," he said.

"Fit to feed an elephant," Jenni said.

Besides Cloning

"You want to close the data center!" Willie almost shouted.

Jenni, Jaque, and Marie had invited the teams working on ASLO to join them individually in the conference room with all the brown paper. Each team had a thirty-minute slot where Jenni, Jaque, and Marie explained their findings—and the idea to become peanut-shaped. On the wall opposite the circles that had now become a peanut was a wall clad in brown paper to capture the feedback of the engineering teams. It was right before lunch, and the feedback wall was plastered with Post-its. Jenni, Jaque, and Marie had planned to collect feedback to ensure the idea was worth pursuing before presenting it to the rest of the management team.

"Marie," Willie said, "I was asking for more funding, not to be erased from the face of the earth."

Marie's face turned red.

"Willie—" Jenni started.

"No," Willie shouted. "I've given my very best to this company, and now you want to shut down everything I've put in place!"

"No one is deciding whether or not to close the data center," Marie said. "We want your feedback on what would happen if we were to close it."

Willie looked firmly into Marie's eyes. "Richard would never have stood for this," he said.

"You know," Shaine said, "we could migrate to one of the larger cloud providers within six months."

Willie looked at Shaine.

"We wouldn't be able to realize the sales price of our infrastructure before everything was migrated," Shaine continued, "so we'd only see the potential gains in the new year."

Willie walked up to Shaine and looked him straight in the eyes.

"Willie, we're the only company that keeps our own infrastructure," Shaine said. "It's more cost-effective to use a third-party provider."

"No third-party provider can deliver the same quality of hosting as we can internally," Willie said.

"What if we were to provide hosting services to other companies," Marie asked, "if we're so good at it?"

Willie pointed at Marie. "She gets it," he said.

"But, are we hosting company," Jenni asked, "or are we an elephant?"

"Elephant or not," Jaque said, "it's worth investigating—either migrating away from the data center or providing hosting services to others if we do keep it."

"Hosting would add to the costs," Shaine said. "We would be competing with large facilities that are more efficient than us."

"We can be efficient," Willie said, "if we have the right hardware."

Marie added a Post-it to the wall, saying, "Provide hosting services to other companies."

Jenni, Jaque, and Marie sat together during lunch to continue discussing.

"If it takes six months to migrate," Jaque said, "it may not be worth it."

"Hosting for other companies will mean we need to expand the data center," Jenni said. "In the short term, it will be a cost increase."

"Plus, we would need to add new kinds of teams," Marie said, "to service our hosting customers."

Lilly was about to sit down next to Marie, but Jenni met her gaze. Lilly turned around.

"What's that about?" Marie asked.

Jenni scoffed.

"Cats fighting," Jaque said.

"Is that what it is?" Marie asked.

"She's gunning for my job," Jenni said.

"Makes sense," Jaque said. "She is a better developer than you and more well liked."

"Jaque!" Marie said.

"Am I wrong, Jenni?" Jaque said.

Jenni picked up her tray and left.

"Dear God," Marie said.

"Am I wrong?" Jaque asked.

"I don't think Lilly wants Jenni's job," Marie said.

"I don't think so either," Jaque said, "but Lilly is competent, well liked, and has a cool head. It makes sense that Jenni would feel threatened."

"But it's great to have a competent member on your team," Marie said.

Jaque looked at her and smiled. "You're telling me that you don't feel threatened by Eric?" he said.

Marie blushed.

"Not a single little piece of you is worried that your competent team member is gunning for your job," Jaque said, elbowing Marie's side.

"I could be worried," she said, "but I choose not to be."

Jaque put his hand on Marie's shoulder. "He's a good man," he said. "He wouldn't steal your thunder."

Marie took a deep breath. Jaque put his arm down.

"I think we should speak to Richard about the peanut," he said.

"Why?" Marie asked.

"The data center was his vision," he said. "He might have a useful opinion about what should happen to it."

After lunch, Marie, Jaque, and Jenni continued to meet with the delivery teams. Jenni was quiet.

"Separating the teams into feature teams and delivery teams isn't going to fix it," Drue said.

"It's about understanding the dependencies between the specific client requests and the features they tie into," Tom said.

"You need competent people that understand both," Ibrahim said.

"If we could clone you, we would," Jason said to him.

"You wish," Ibrahim said.

"Since we can't clone Ibrahim," Marie said, "how could we create coherence between the specific client configuration and the platform itself?"

Ibrahim grabbed a marker and went to the brown paper with the circles on it. "You see these teams here?" he said, pointing at the delivery teams. "They don't just create new features. They create versions of those features before they're integrated back into the platform." He drew an arrow back to a feature circle. Then another one next to it. Then another. "When another team creates a similar feature," he drew an arrow from a different delivery circle back to the same feature circle, "there isn't just one conflict to resolve, but several, on already-live applications being used by clients."

"That's why our hosting is exploding in size," Tom said. "We're running duplicative processes."

Marie looked over at Jenni.

"How do we adjudicate these changes?" Jenni asked.

"We used to talk—and fight—about these things during our daily stand-ups," Ibrahim said, "but someone thought that they weren't a productive use of our time."

Jenni looked away.

"How many of these duplicative lines do we have?" Jaque asked.

Ibrahim looked at the board.

"We have many per customer," Jason answered. "It's gotten worse in the months I've been gone."

"It has gotten unmanageable since Anne left," Ibrahim said.

"That's what she was doing in all those meetings," Jenni said. "Trimming the lines." She got up and left the room, closing the door behind her.

Marie looked over at Jaque.

"Ibra," Jaque said, "can this be fixed?"

Ibrahim shook his head. "I think we need to rebuild," he said.

Jaque looked over at Jason.

"We could still try to untangle these changes," Jason said, "but we would need to change how we operate. We need to kill off the delivery teams and focus on getting the platform into better shape."

"Or the technical debt will kill us," said Tom.

"I don't think we need to move all the delivery people into feature teams," Drue said. "We could have a customer-facing team, but they shouldn't be allowed to change anything in the actual platform. Any changes would need to be coordinated and discussed with the team responsible for the feature."

"That will give a worse customer experience," Jaque said.

"But a more stable platform," Jason said.

"I'm not sure changing the team structure is going to help," Tom said. "As I mentioned before, when the delivery and platform work well in unison, it's usually because people manage to communicate well together. Moving people around into a new structure isn't going to help."

"It's about our culture," Marie said.

After the last engineers left, Jaque and Marie were alone in the conference room.

"Where did Jenni go?" Jaque asked.

Marie shrugged. They both sat on the conference table looking at the Post-its that captured the feedback from the teams.

"This does give a good overview," Jaque said. He walked up to the board. "Look, these notes here—they're all about the data center and how we either need to invest more in it or get rid of it." He moved Post-its around so that there was a clear cluster about the data center.

"These here," he continued, "are about our pricing structure. We charge too little for our product and don't explain the value-add our customers currently get beyond the initial purchase."

"And these here," he said, pointing to the remainder, "are all about how to organize our teams."

"What's your summary of those?" Marie asked.

"That what we're doing right now is definitely not working," he said.

Marie laughed. "I agree," she said, "Also, maybe it's not a structural problem, and it's more a problem about people not communicating sufficiently with each other."

"I'll write up the business cases for the price restructuring and look further into the data center," Jaque said. "The organization of the teams I'll leave in your capable hands."

The Hard Stuff

Marie found Jenni sitting at the bottom of the stairwell. Marie sat down next to her and asked, "Why did you leave?"

Jenni did not move. Marie sat in silence.

"I think I liked it better when it was a mess down here," Jenni said.

Marie chuckled. "It had its charm," Marie said.

"When everything's out in the open," Jenni said, "you can't help but see things clearly."

"What kind of things are you talking about?" Marie asked.

"I unraveled ASLO. Whatever threads were holding it together, I removed them," Jenni said.

"To be fair," Marie said, "perhaps being held together by threads was structurally unsound."

Jenni smiled faintly. "I focused on efficiency," Jenni said. "We needed to focus on resolving the quality, not on how fast we could get to poor quality."

"It wasn't just you," Marie said. "You were under a lot of pressure from Natalie."

"I should have protected my teams from that pressure, not passed it on," Jenni said. "I don't know how to restructure the teams so that it makes more sense."

"I don't think there is a right answer to that," Marie said. "I think that we need to focus on giving people a sense of responsibility so that they can find the right way to organize."

"You mean, start with the culture," Jenni said.

Marie smiled.

Waiting to meet Anne, Marie was nervous. She felt like she was doing something wrong. But, if a solution already existed, she wanted to get her hands on it.

"Hi, Marie," Anne said.

Marie got up to give Anne a hug.

"Oh, we're hugging now," Anne said, patting Marie on the back from an arm's length.

Marie pointed at the teapot and cinnamon buns already served at their usual table at the coffee shop.

"We're going to need more of those," Anne said. "I've invited the whole gang."

Marie could feel her cheeks warm up. Why would Anne invite more people when it was hard enough to speak with her?

Jaque sat down.

"You just follow me wherever I go," Marie said.

"I won't eat your bun this time," Jaque said. "Anne gave me a stern talking to."

"You were being disrespectful," Anne said, her face motionless.

"I was being playful," Jaque said.

"Thin line, Jaque," Anne said.

Marie was surprised that Anne came to her defense.

"I'll order more buns," Jaque said, "and respect Marie's boundaries." He winked at Marie and went to the counter.

"You can tell him how you feel," Anne said. "He comes off rude, but he's actually a good person."

"Hey," Jason said and sat down.

"Jason!" Marie said and put a hand on his shoulder.

"May I join you?" a deep male voice said behind Marie.

Marie turned around to find both Richard and Simon there.

"I brought a friend," Richard said.

"I hear you're killing off the data center," Simon said. "Only my life's work."

"News travels fast," Marie said, looking at Richard. "I hope this doesn't ruin our chances of being acquired."

"This is strictly between friends," Richard said.

Jaque arrived at the table with a stack of cinnamon buns. "Richard," he said, attempting to shake his hand while holding all his orders.

"I just wanted to speak with Anne about how she had envisioned the ASLO teams should be organized,"

Marie said. "I don't know what everyone else has in mind?"

"It's all part of the system," Anne said. "The engineering teams, the pricing structure, the data center."

"Time is running out," Jaque said. "We need to find a way to keep ASLO alive and our people employed beyond Christmas."

"The 'we' here is this group?" Marie asked.

"It sure isn't my leadership team at Zebra," Jaque said.

"Doesn't that seem wrong to you?" Marie said.

"Marie, you may be able to inspire change in our engineering teams," Jaque said, "and I'm impressed by how far you've come with Jenni—she's had a total change of heart—but I don't think you stand a chance with Natalie."

"I may not be able to do much," Marie said, "but I might just know the person who can."

Richard met her gaze. "I might have been able to before," Richard said, "but I don't think I command her trust anymore."

"Richard," Jaque said, "why did you insist on having an in-house data center?"

"My vision was to create advanced learning experiences that would capture kids' attention as much as video games. It was a matter of taking responsibility for all the links in the chain," Richard said, "and making sure that we're good at every part of it." He looked down. "I'm not sure I would have made the same decision today. The quality of service with other cloud providers is much better now than when we built ASLO. Maybe today, we would have stored it in a third-party cloud to begin with."

"Now you tell me," Simon said.

"You don't even work in hardware anymore," Richard said.

"Only because ConvoSystems doesn't have any hardware," Simon said.

"The question isn't what's important for Richard or Simon," Anne interrupted. "The question is, what is the right thing to do for ASLO and Zebra."

"I don't think we're dependent on having our own data center," Jason said.

"The initial numbers from Aysha show that, in the first year, moving to a cloud-based service has a significant upfront investment, but that it pays back in three years—and has significant cost savings after that," Jaque said.

"Does that account for the revenue we could get from selling off the equipment in the data center?" Jason asked.

"Unfortunately, it does," Jaque said. "We haven't upgraded our equipment in a long time."

"You could create a different pricing structure for ASLO," Anne said. "I tried to pitch that to Natalie."

"Natalie always wanted the cash now," Richard said.

"I would like to see your calculations on that, Anne," Jaque said.

"Sure, let's go over them," Anne said. "Do you want to meet here tomorrow?"

Marie started shifting in her seat. Finally, she couldn't take it anymore. "This was supposed to be my afternoon with Anne," she said. "I wanted to try to figure out how we could structure our teams differently to avoid the architectural mess we find ourselves in." Marie looked around.

"Marie," Richard said, "it's a mess because there are many points of failure."

"That's why I invited everyone," Anne said. "You need to hear all the perspectives."

"I tried to embed a sense of responsibility in each of the developers," Richard said, "which is why I was against getting dedicated people in the team to manage the group dynamics."

"That's backfired now, Richard," Jason said.

"I didn't anticipate leaving Zebra and not being in control of what kinds of metrics the teams would be measured on," Richard said.

"I tried to make sure that all the teams still understood what the other teams were doing," Anne said, "but it became unsustainable when I was the only person doing that."

"I was protecting the hardware folks over everyone else's needs," Simon said, "because they were my responsibility."

"The whole product was your responsibility," Richard said.

"That's not how it feels when you're being asked to squeeze every ounce of efficiency out of your people," Simon said. "Then, you protect your people."

"We need these teams thinking and communicating again," Jaque said, "or we're going to start losing customers, and our end will come even earlier."

"You shouldn't re-organize," Anne said, "but you do need to work on both the product and the delivery."

"Thanks, Anne," Marie said and rolled her eyes.

"You could dedicate a small team of people to working on the platform—to at least understand the amount of technical debt we have," Anne said. "And you could dedicate a small team of people to take ownership of speaking to the other teams and figuring out what's going on."

"I could be one of those people," Jason suggested.

Marie smiled at him.

"And you need to keep telling them that the whole product is their responsibility," Richard said to Marie, with a sideward glance at Simon.

"Happy now?" Anne asked.

"Grudgingly happy," Marie said.

The Whole Product

Jenni agreed to dedicate one team to investigating the amount of technical debt, and she also agreed to appoint individuals to act as "strings" to hold the delivery teams together.

Marie was walking down the hallway in the engineering department when she met Ibrahim, wheeling a whiteboard. "Where are you going with that?" Marie asked.

"I'm revolting," Ibrahim said, "and putting this in my office."

"Why is that a revolt?" Marie asked.

"Because I'll stop maintaining the Jira board for my delivery team," he said with a smile.

"Won't that make it harder for other teams to know what you're up to?" she asked.

"The other teams will need to walk their asses into my actual office to look at my board," Ibrahim said, "so they can ask questions and understand the context of what we're doing."

"Who is your string?" Marie asked.

"Technically, we're all strings, Marie," Ibrahim said, "but Drue will be the one with formal responsibility for snooping on the other teams."

"You're right," Marie said, "ideally everyone would be strings."

"Hey," Ibrahim said, "getting Jenni to let go of even some of her madness is pretty impressive."

Marie smiled.

"We'll take it from here," Ibrahim said and wheeled on.

Marie felt her stomach turn. Who was "we" in this scenario?

Later, Marie was having lunch with Eric and Sheila when Natalie sat down next to her.

"They've stopped reporting on their quality numbers," Natalie said, biting into a whole sausage.

"Who?" Marie asked.

"A couple of the engineering teams," Natalie said, taking a big bite of her bread. "Your HR magic is impacting my numbers, Marie."

"But is the quality actually improving?" Marie asked.

Natalie turned her whole body toward Marie. "I don't know," she said.

Marie thought about Ibrahim's whiteboard. There was no getting numbers from that into Natalie's spreadsheet.

"And you know the worst thing?" Natalie continued.

Marie shook her head.

"Jenni is starting to sound just like Anne," Natalie said. She gulped down the rest of her meal and left without another word.

"Stirring the pot in engineering, Marie?" Eric asked.

"I might have a bit less power than you attributed to me," Marie said.

"You'll get this right in the end," Sheila said. "You always do."

"I hope so," Marie said. She looked down at her plate. When she looked up, she saw Willie walking past her. He caught her gaze and deliberately looked away. "I really hope so," she said, "before it's too late."

Flying Blind

Marie was pacing outside of the conference center on the ground floor. To address ASLO's quality issues, she and the engineers had arranged an advisory board of parents and teachers. It was early afternoon.

"Hey, Marie," a voice said from behind her.

Marie turned around and saw Andrea. "Oh, hey," Marie said, "I haven't seen you in a long time."

"Jaque has me calculating different scenarios for what we can do with the data center," Andrea said.

"Which one is in the lead?" Marie asked.

"None of them are great," Andrea said.

Marie looked at her. "Are you OK with the court proceedings?" Marie asked.

Andrea gave a half-smile. "I'm OK," she said.

Marie opened her mouth and was tempted to ask all her questions about what was happening between Frank and Andrea and why they were in court in the first place, but she managed to compose herself.

"Look," Andrea said, "we will move past this. I will move past it. If it were up to me alone, I would have just let this whole thing stay in Moscow."

"So you did travel to Russia with Frank and Natalie?" Marie said, her jaw dropping.

Andrea frowned her brows. "Yes," she said, "I was the lead analyst on the case for whether we should import elements for the data center from Russia."

"Of course you were," Marie said, considering whether that sounded patronizing.

"I didn't even see him interacting with the Russians," Andrea said. "I only know what he told me afterward in the bar."

Marie's eyes grew wide. This was not at all what she had assumed the court case was about. She thought that Frank had been inappropriate about Andrea's transition. Marie could feel her cheeks blush.

"I had no choice but to go to Natalie," Andrea said. "If Frank had just owned up to what he did and not tried to discredit me, we wouldn't need to be in court right now."

"I …" Marie started.

Andrea tilted her face. "I assumed Paul had told you this," Andrea said, "but you seem surprised."

"Paul hasn't told me anything," Marie said, "and neither has Mark."

Andrea looked down. "Look," she said, "my take is that Frank was doing what he thought was best for Zebra. He loves this company."

"He's built a transparent and well-functioning finance team. Why would he attempt to do shady deals with the Russians?" Marie said.

Andrea looked at Marie. "People are neither wholly good nor bad; wholly competent or incompetent. We're all trying to be the best versions of ourselves," Andrea said. "I mean, I should now." She gestured to her body.

Marie nodded hesitantly as she heard footsteps approaching. A woman in a floral dress was walking toward her.

"Hi, are you here for the advisory board?" Marie asked and gestured for the woman to follow the signs to the conference room.

When Marie turned back around, she saw Andrea walking down the corridor toward the staircase. Marie felt a pull to follow her, but she planted her feet and waited for more advisory board members to arrive.

Two days later, Jenni, Jaque, Mark, and Natalie were all sitting in the same conference room where the advisory board had been hosted. The posters from the meeting were still on the walls. Jason and Jo were handing out Post-it notes when Marie entered.

"I don't know how I feel about that sad smiley face over there," Natalie said, pointing to one of the posters.

"All in good time," Jo said, gesturing for Natalie to sit down.

Jason stood in front of the big TV screen in the room and closed the door. He turned toward the group. "As you know, we conducted an advisory board to understand exactly what's happening when users interact with ASLO," he said.

"We had representatives from both the teachers' and the parents' sides," Jo said from the back of the room. "Everyone used to love ASLO," Jo continued, "so there was a lot of frustration in the room."

"What are they frustrated with?" Natalie asked.

"Everything," Jo said.

"Let's look at some of the major frustration points," Jason said, walking over to a poster. "ASLO is slow," he said, pointing to one of the clusters of Post-its. "It's buggy and crashes often. Teachers find it hard to create a coherent learning progression plan."

"And according to the parents, it has become harder to maintain their kids' focus on doing their lesson plan," Jo said.

Natalie stood up and walked over to Jason. She read the notes in each cluster, touching them with her fingertips. She put her forehead against the wall. The room was quiet. Natalie turned around. "It's not just the UX," she sighed. She pointed at the first two clusters of notes. "It's our code," she said. Then, she pointed toward the second of the two clusters. "But it's also the soul of our product," she said. "It's the design of the learning experience."

Natalie sat down on the floor next to the poster. "I need to talk to Mark," she said, looking around the room. "Everyone else, please leave."

Marie looked around. She caught Mark's gaze. He smiled at her and nodded toward the door.

While Natalie and Mark spoke, Jenni, Jaque, and Marie got coffee in the conference center kitchen. Jo and Jason sat down in an adjacent conference room to prepare to send out a user survey to firm up the observations they had gathered from the advisory board.

"What was that about?" Marie asked.

"She relies on Mark a lot," Jaque said.

"She's a teacher," Jenni said. "If our products are failing in teaching, that must feel like a personal failure."

"How is the quality of our product trending?" Marie asked.

Jenni scoffed. "You may be best positioned to answer that," Jenni said.

Marie raised an eyebrow.

"It's all on your boards now," Jenni said, shaking her head.

"Let's just dwell on the fact that you're head of engineering, Jenni," Jaque said. "You're accountable for our product."

Jenni furrowed her eyebrows.

"I don't know about the quality of the code or whether it's better integrated," Marie said, "but our new setup with strings ensuring that teams talk to each other seems to be working. Drue was telling me that they identified two features being implemented that would have canceled each other out."

Jenni looked toward the conference room. "How long do you think they'll be in there?" Jenni asked.

Jaque shrugged.

Shaine walked into the kitchen. He looked around. "Is this a meeting?" he asked.

"No, go ahead," Marie said, moving away from the coffee machine.

"It might be a while," Jaque said, nodding toward the conference room.

"You know," Shaine said, "I've been thinking about our data center."

"Yes?" Jenni said and raised her eyebrows.

"Why don't we pivot into supporting large language model calculations?" he said, "You know, for generative AI."

"That sounds like the same scenario as renting the data center out to other companies that you and Andrea are already looking into," Jaque said.

"It's not quite the same," Shaine said. "This would be a specialization of the data center—using the segregation that we already have in place for schools to ensure that their data doesn't get intertwined, but providing it to health technology companies, for example."

Jaque's eyes widened.

"Then it would actually be of benefit that we've created this monstrously secure and completely redundant data center," Shaine said.

Jenni nodded and touched her chin with her hand. "That's actually a good point," she said.

Shaine looked at Marie. "I'm telling you, no one knows what I can do," he said.

"You're a cracker, Shaine," Jaque said, "but I do want to understand more about this idea. Do you have time now?"

"Sure," Shaine said. He picked up his coffee cup from the machine.

Jaque grabbed Jenni by the shoulder. "I need you for this, too," he said. Jenni followed the movement of his hand out of the kitchenette.

Marie finished her coffee and decided to check in on Mark and Natalie. She passed the meeting room and looked through the glass window next to the door. Mark was lying back in a chair while Natalie paced back and forth across the room. Mark was nodding. He caught Marie's gaze and shook his head slightly from side to side. Marie took it as an indication that the advisory board debrief meeting was over. For good.

Species

Marie was waiting in line at the coffee shop. It was Thursday morning, and she was feeling on edge. It felt like everything at Zebra was shifting. She was having a hard time figuring out what to hold on to. She didn't have her position as head of HR development to prop her up. The culture initiative that was supposed to have been implemented by now had changed character. The engineers were doing better at working together, though. From what she could tell, the quality of ASLO was also improving. But, none of it would matter if ASLO stopped making a difference or the company's profitability didn't improve.

Marie felt a hand on her shoulder. She turned around.

"Hi, Todd," she said and gave him a hug.

"How are things?" he asked.

Marie paused and moved to the side, out of the line. Todd followed her.

"You know," she said, "things are difficult right now."

"I heard some of that," he said.

Marie lifted her eyebrows.

"But, you know," he said, "things aren't always easy on our post-transformation side either."

"How so?" Marie asked. "I thought you guys had achieved organizational nirvana."

Todd chuckled. "There is no steady state in an organization," Todd said. "It all depends on the people who work there."

"I guess you're right," Marie said.

"Since Richard joined," Todd said, "things have started to get more difficult."

"What?" Marie said and opened her mouth. "But he gels with your values perfectly."

"Indeed," Todd said, "but his vision for our technology is somewhat at odds with how we've built the company. He likes to own and control the full value chain."

Marie smiled. "Yes," she said, "that's why we have a data center at Zebra."

"Well, if we're not careful," Todd said, "we might end up having a data center at ConvoSystems."

"Data centers are their own type of animal," Marie said.

"They may be a zebra," Todd said.

"You have our former Zebra," Marie said.

"He might prefer to be yours," Todd said.

Marie and Todd looked at each other.

"I was naive, you know," Marie said.

"Yes, you were," Todd said with a grin.

"Wait," Marie said, "what are you talking about?"

"I was naive too," Todd said, "thinking that transforming ConvoSystems to be a more human-friendly workplace would be the end of the road."

"It seems more like a beginning," Marie said.

"And the end is unknown," Todd said. Todd put a hand on Marie's shoulder. Marie could feel her eyes moistening. "Shall we order?" he asked, and they both got back in line.

Jaque was sitting in Marie's chair when she came into her shared office with the engineers.

"Coming in at a leisurely hour, are we?" he asked.

"I had coffee with Todd from ConvoSystems," she said.

"Coffee with our potential buyers?" Ibrahim said.

"Did you speak to Richard?" Jason asked.

"No, I just ran into Todd," Marie replied.

"We need Richard back," Jason said.

"He might need us back, too," Marie said.

Jaque got up from Marie's chair. "It might actually work," Jaque said.

"What might work?" Marie asked.

"Shaine's idea of selling our GPU to LLM processing," Jaque said.

"Oh?" Marie said.

"It's as if Richard and Simon designed the data center for this exact purpose," Jaque said, "even though they wouldn't have had any idea what LLM would become when they designed it."

"Richard did have a vision of what AI could do for learning," Ibrahim said. "He would go on about it after a couple of beers." Ibrahim laughed. "That's when Natalie would start rolling her eyes and call it a night." He sighed.

"I miss those days when we were just a couple of developers working odd hours and having drinks at even odder hours," Drue said.

Ibrahim exhaled.

Marie looked at Jaque. "Would that make the strongest business case for what we should do with the data center?" she asked. "Spin it out as a separate service and host ASLO on a third-party cloud?"

"There is an element of timing in it," Jaque said. "We would need to host ASLO in our own data center until it's profitable enough to pay for the switch to a third-party cloud." Jaque took a deep breath. "Once ASLO is migrated," he said, "there really is no common denominator between the data center and ASLO."

"They're separate animals altogether," Marie said.

"The question is," Jaque said, "which one is a Zebra?"

During Friday breakfast, Marie was biting into a bun when Shaine came to sit with her.

"I can't believe how many people are into cinnamon buns," Shaine said.

Marie chewed as quickly as she could. "I don't think it's the buns specifically," she said. "It's about having some sort of ritual."

"Isn't lunch a ritual?" he said. "I mean, we do the same thing as at Friday breakfast. Everyone meets up in the canteen and eats. Except we do it every day at noon rather than on Friday mornings."

"I see your point," she said.

"I liked the secret bun meet-ups that we had upstairs," Shaine said. "This feels more corporate."

"Do you think efficiency takes away from the ritual?" Marie asked. "I mean, this way, we're not excluding anyone or only hanging out in our departmental silos."

"It's not straightforward," Shaine said. He pointed his head in the direction of the stairwell to the basement. "That mess of a basement was also an institution when I arrived here," he said. "We're all better off for it being cleaned up now."

Marie smiled. "I was happy that you and Willie did that together," she said.

"You're all warm and fuzzy for collaboration," Shaine smirked. "Typical HR."

"Have you talked to him recently?" Marie asked.

"Willie?" Shaine asked.

"Yeah, he won't even look at me these days," Marie said.

"I've spoken to him," Shaine said. "He has big news." Shaine smiled. "He's auditioned for a role in a play."

"What!" Marie exclaimed. "That man keeps amazing me."

"Apparently, it's a paid gig, too," Shaine said. "He must really know his stuff."

Marie's smile suddenly faded. Could they be losing Willie to the arts?

The Second Coming

On Monday morning, Marie was looking for Mark. He wasn't in his office. He wasn't in Natalie's office. He wasn't in the kitchenette. The whole executive floor was empty. Finally, Marie checked the conference center. She found Natalie and Jason drawing on a whiteboard. Neither Jason nor Natalie noticed her peeking through the window to the conference room.

"She's decided to fix it," Mark said.

Marie's shoulders jumped to her ears, and she turned around. "Jesus," she said, "you startled me."

"That's what she decided last week," Mark sighed.

"To fix what?" Marie asked.

"The whole thing," Mark said. "The UX of ASLO, the learning paths for students, the teaching experience."

"We have the content design team for that," Marie said.

"Natalie built our first products herself," Mark said.

"I assumed Richard built them," Marie said.

"He coded them, yes," Mark said, "but she designed them—with teachers and students in mind."

"But she didn't build ASLO," Marie said. "Anne designed it."

"And that is what Natalie thinks is wrong with ASLO," Mark said. "That Anne did it wrong."

"Clearly, she didn't," Marie said. "ASLO is our most successful product."

"Well, to Natalie, that feels like a loss of control over the company," Mark said.

"I can see that," Marie said. "When you do everything, you understand everything."

"But, if you're the CEO, your primary job is to lead the people who understand everything," Mark said. He shrugged his shoulders. "I don't know how else to explain it," Mark said.

Marie looked at him. "How are you?" she asked.

He sighed. "I'm tired, Marie," he said.

"Having trouble sleeping?" she asked.

"No," he said, "I'm tired of trying to mold Natalie into a CEO."

Marie raised her eyebrows.

"That's my main job here," he said, "or at least it has become so." He gestured toward the conference center. "And now she's hellbent on being a product designer."

"Maybe that's the kind of animal she is," Marie said.

"Maybe," he said, "but someone needs to lead this company. And that someone just abdicated." Mark looked at Marie. "When are you coming back to the HR floor?" he asked.

"I'm not sure," Marie said. "It seems like one issue leads to another these days, and I find myself wondering whether I'm making any difference at all."

"Eric isn't you," Mark said. "He does a good job with Jo and Sheila; he really notices the team. But he doesn't notice the people who need the team's expertise."

Marie widened her eyes.

"It's OK for now," Mark said, putting a hand on her shoulder, "but he's no you."

Later, Marie was filling her lunch plate at the buffet. Joseph was standing in front of the door to the kitchen. He rose up on his toes to look at her plate. Marie gave a half-smile, and he smiled back.

Marie sat down at a table where Eric and Lilly were sitting.

"The new way of working is, well, working," Lilly said, looking at Marie.

"I'm happy to hear that," Marie said.

"In my team, we've picked a value to focus on for this sprint," Lilly said.

"Like a goal for a sprint that is a value?" Eric asked.

"Yeah," Lilly said, "we were talking about how to get the team to feel more like when Richard was here.

What Richard did a lot was talk about not just the work but how we were doing the work."

"So, which value did you pick for this sprint?" Marie asked.

"We picked curiosity," Lilly said, "because we need to be curious about what's happening with the code right now and apply a scientist's mindset. Otherwise, it's easy to blame the other teams for all the bugs currently in there."

"Are there still many bugs?" Eric asked.

"I've never seen a system malfunctioning in so many ways," Lilly said. "It is curious, really."

After lunch, Marie returned to her office. Drue and Ibrahim were at their desks.

"Have you heard that Lilly's team has adopted value goals for their sprints?" she asked them.

"They totally stole that from us," Ibrahim said. He looked over at Drue. "Those strings that travel between the teams spread all the gossip," he said.

"Some places would call that spreading good practice," Drue said.

"What value goal does your team have right now?" Marie asked.

"It's *our* team, Marie. You're part of it," Drue said.

"She isn't really, though," Ibrahim said.

"I know I don't attend all ceremonies," Marie said.

"You're no good at coding anyway," Drue said.

"Our goal is commitment," Ibrahim said, "because someone on the team is more focused on brand-new shiny things than on fixing what we have."

Ibrahim nodded toward Shaine's desk.

"His brand-new, shiny idea may help the company," Drue said.

"Yeah, right," Ibrahim said.

"How does Jenni feel about the new value goals?" Marie asked.

Drue and Ibrahim looked at each other. "I don't think anyone has told her," Ibrahim said.

Marie frowned.

That Friday, Jaque had arranged a full-day meeting for Jenni, Natalie, Mark, and Marie to go over opportunities for revising the pricing structure as well as cases for turning the data center into a profit center. Andrea and Shaine would present the business cases. Aysha would present the current state of Zebra's finances.

Marie was eating a croissant when Jenni came to join her at her table.

"Did you hear what Lilly's done?" Jenni said as she sat down.

Marie shook her head.

"She's changed the sprint goals," Jenni said. "Now the teams pursue value goals per sprint, not actual delivery goals." Jenni started stirring her coffee as if she was attempting to make a tornado in it.

"I've heard about this," Marie said.

"Of course you have," Jenni said. "Are you going to tell me this was your idea?"

"No," Marie said, leaning back in her seat to avoid the potential coffee splash zone. "It was Ibrahim's idea, and then some of the other teams adopted the practice as well."

"I'm sure it was Lilly," Jenni said. She pushed her coffee cup away. "She does everything she can to undermine me."

"I'm not sure I see how this undermines you," Marie said.

"They've changed what they measure in the sprints without discussing it with me first," Jenni said, standing up.

"Jenni," Marie said, "as far as I understand, the value goal is an additional focus area and not a replacement for delivery goals."

"It doesn't matter," Jenni said. "They should have talked to me."

"I don't dispute that," Marie said.

"But did you talk to them?" a deep voice said.

Marie looked behind Jenni and saw a tall man with a long white beard and wearing a light gray suit. Richard sat down in the chair Jenni had just left.

"Richard," Jenni said without looking at him.

"Jenni," Richard said, extending his arm toward her.

Jenni looked straight ahead for a couple of beats. Then she turned toward him and shook his hand without meeting his gaze.

"I didn't know you would be here," Marie said.

"Natalie invited me," Richard said, "as a special guest."

"As an investor?" Marie asked.

Richard shrugged. "I got the call last night," he said. "I had to clear my whole schedule today on short notice."

"But you just had to come …" Jenni said.

"I have to aid the company that I built," Richard said, "if having values as sprint goals has become a mortal sin."

Jenni shook her head and walked away.

Richard laughed softly. "Natalie wasn't kidding about that one," he said, following Jenni with his gaze.

Marie leaned in over the table. "Why are you here, Richard?" she asked.

"Natalie and I had started something good," he said, "and we let money concerns take it away from us—from both of us—and now it may die." He put his hands in front of him. "The least I can do is try to inject whatever creative power I have to make sure it lives."

"It's your second coming," Marie said.

Richard smiled, and the sun shone on him through the window as the clouds parted outside.

If We All Stand Together

"Richard," Jaque said, lifting his eyebrows, as Richard and Marie entered the conference room.

Natalie walked over to Richard and opened her arms. He pulled her in and held her head to his chest with his hand.

"I'm so glad you called," he said.

Natalie took a step back, out of Richard's embrace.

Mark extended his arm to Richard.

"You've done well," Richard said.

"With what?" Mark asked.

"With Natalie," Richard said.

Mark lifted an eyebrow.

"I don't think you've met Andrea and Shaine," Natalie said, taking Richard by the elbow and walking him over to the corner of the room.

"I've heard a lot about you, Richard," Andrea said as she shook his hand.

"You and I seem to have passed each other when we changed employers," Shaine said. "I recently joined from ConvoSystems."

"And yet it feels like you've been here forever," Jaque said.

Shaine frowned.

"When will Aysha be here?" Natalie asked.

"I asked her to give us the morning to go over the options," Jaque said, "then she can come and kill our dreams with financial reality in the afternoon."

"You're in charge of finance now?" Richard asked.

"I'm not sure that's entirely accurate," Jaque said. "They're pretty much in charge of themselves."

"That is how Frank built it," Richard said, a glimmer in his eye.

Jaque looked at Natalie. Then at Richard. "Why is he here?" Jaque asked.

"I asked him to join us," Natalie said.

"How do you intend him to participate?" Jaque asked.

"I want his opinion," Natalie said.

"As a potential investor?" Jaque asked.

"As a founder of this company," Natalie said.

"Has he signed an NDA?" Jaque asked.

Natalie looked at Richard.

"I have, as part of our previous conversations," Richard said.

"Is that the same capacity that you're here in now?" Jaque asked. "As part of your job at ConvoSystems?"

"Jaque," Natalie said.

"I don't want to jeopardize any of the possibilities we discuss due to rumors of our situation spreading," Jaque said.

Natalie frowned.

"It's only been a couple of months since you were considering suing him," Jaque said.

"You were going to sue me?" Richard asked.

Natalie looked at her feet. "I didn't sue you, though," she said.

"No," he said, "not yet." He burst into thunderous laughter.

Jaque looked from Natalie to Richard.

"How about we consider ourselves covered by the terms in our NDAs with ConvoSystems," Mark said.

"It's not my intention to divulge any information about Zebra Apps," Richard said. "I'm here as a parent whose child needs advice."

"A child of whom you have no legal custody," Jaque said.

Richard smirked.

"Shall we begin?" Jaque said. He walked over to the whiteboard and picked up a marker. He wrote on the board:

Why are we here?

"We will decide what course of action to take given our problems and options," Jaque said.

"So, we are deciding that today?" Mark said, looking over at Natalie.

"This's why I wanted Richard here," Natalie said.

"Shouldn't we include the findings that Jo and Jason collected from the advisory board and user survey?" Marie asked.

"We've accounted for their findings in our scenarios," Andrea said.

"Let's start by walking through the problems we're facing," Jaque said.

He walked over to the wall opposite the windows. A number of meeting charts were attached to the wall, with blank meeting charts hanging over them, hiding the content underneath.

Jaque revealed the first chart.

"The symptoms of our problems are discontented users and a fall in new sales and contract renewals," Jaque said, "which translates directly to our current financial situation." Jaque looked around. "No spoilers, but it's not where we want it to be. We've tracked these problems to three main root causes," he said as he revealed the next meeting chart. "Our pricing structure only funds the delivery of new solutions, not platform enhancements or the data center." He paused and looked around. People in the room were nodding. "The quality of our product has decreased considerably because our teams stopped working together across customer silos."

Natalie walked up and stood next to Jaque. "And our customers no longer perceive ASLO as their first choice of product because it fails to support them in creating the learning journeys and experiences that we have always been known for," she said.

Jaque looked at Natalie. "That was actually not my third point," he said.

"Maybe it should be," Natalie said. "If our flagship product doesn't enhance learning, what are we doing as an edtech company."

"What was your number three?" Richard asked Jaque.

"It's the state of the data center," Jaque said.

"What is its state?" Richard asked.

"We're failing to scale it to the customer uptick that we have, even if it is meager," Jaque said, "due to our current pricing model. And because of the current state of ASLO's code, every feature upgrade occupies a disproportionate amount of space."

Richard looked at Natalie. "There's no funding for the data center?" Richard asked.

"We've focused our pricing model on keeping long-term costs down for our users," Natalie said.

Richard scratched his beard.

"I believe we all agreed to this," Mark said.

"We've also addressed some of these issues," Jenni said, "and we're seeing improvements in product quality as the teams work together more closely."

"Yes," Marie said, "the strings that wander between the teams not only spread information, they also spread best practices."

"Like the value goals?" Richard asked.

"Yes," Marie said.

Jenni's face turned red.

"There have been examples of the teams identifying conflicting changes that could have created further problems in the code base," Marie said.

"We're flying blind, though," Jenni said. "We've lost all visibility of the quality metrics."

"Not all quality metrics," Marie said. "We have metrics on a team level on their boards."

Jenni looked at Marie.

"Is the product better?" Richard asked.

"The newest release was better received than the previous one," Jaque said, "but my sales teams are still being met with questions about why the product has become so difficult to use."

"Yeah," Marie said, "that's what I hear from the engineers who have children in schools where they use ASLO. People are happy it's less horrible than the last release but are still considering whether it's worth the investment."

"The user survey Jo and Jason did shows the same trend," Andrea said. "Our users have stayed with us out of a sense of loyalty, but many are starting to consider alternative options."

Richard looked at Andrea. "Alternative options?" he said.

"We're no longer the only player in this field," Jaque said. "Many other companies have caught up with the trend of using classroom time for teacher–pupil interaction and delivering instruction as homework."

"We have four key problems that are the reasons for the poor financial situation that we're in," Mark said.

Jaque looked at Mark. Then at Natalie.

"Yes," he said, "four." He wrote Natalie's point about the difficulty of designing training plans in the systems as a fourth bullet on the poster.

Andrea stood up. She and Shaine walked to the front of the room, and Jaque sat down.

"We've taken a closer look at scenarios generated by the teams," Shaine said.

"They needed a more careful look than the restructuring already implemented," Andrea said.

"Are we doing team restructuring carelessly?" Jenni said.

"It was safe enough to try," Marie said, "without much consequence for anyone else."

"You clearly didn't consult with everyone who needs to be represented to make company-wide product decisions," Mark said.

"We didn't," Jaque said. "That's why you're being presented with the analysis right now." Jaque looked at Mark.

Mark looked at Natalie. Natalie looked straight ahead.

"Let's review the scenarios," Andrea said.

"I would like to know which scenarios we're going to review," Mark said.

Andrea looked at Jaque. He nodded. "Like a table of contents?" Andrea asked.

"That's the first slide," Shaine said and clicked to change the slide.

"We have two main areas we want to address," Andrea said, pointing to the slide. "As you can see, we're assuming that all scenarios are based on us splitting the product side and the data center."

"Is that a certainty?" Mark asked.

"There are few dependencies between the two," Jaque said.

"Wait a minute," Richard said, "you're saying that the data center is not needed for ASLO?"

"That's exactly what we're saying," Shaine said. "We're also saying that the data center is an asset that can be capitalized on."

Richard leaned forward in his seat. Shaine clicked to the next slide.

"For the data center, we have the following scenarios," Andrea continued. "We can sell the spare parts and rent out the space, basically capitalizing on the individual physical components."

"You want to sell it for parts?" Richard said loudly and sprang up from his chair.

"That's one scenario," Shaine said.

"Richard," Jaque said, "let's wait to evaluate the scenarios. Right now, just take in the analysis."

Richard looked at Natalie. She nodded, and he sat down.

"We can also rent out the storage space from the data center to other companies, essentially becoming a data storage provider," Andrea continued. "Lastly, we could spin out the data center as a separate company, using the current storage division built into our data center, and become a partner to companies building large language models, especially health tech companies."

Richard nodded.

"This is true," he said. "I had always imagined that any sort of AI capability would require data separation."

"It's as if you built the data center for this purpose," Shaine said.

"We could also provide solutions ourselves," Richard said, "based on the data center infrastructure."

"That's true," Andrea said, "but we didn't include that scenario since it would require significant investment."

"In all scenarios, though," Mark said, "you assume that ASLO is stored elsewhere."

"Yes," Shaine said, "in all our calculations, moving ASLO to a more cost-efficient hosting provider will make ASLO more profitable."

"And it'll help us scale ASLO to avoid the slowness that our users are currently experiencing," Andrea said.

There was a knock on the door. Jaque got up to see who it was. It was a waiter who whispered to Jaque, "They're about to clear the lunch buffet."

"It's 1 p.m. already," Mark said, looking at his watch.

"Do you feel like breaking for lunch now or continuing with the scenarios?" Andrea asked.

"Let's continue with the scenarios," Natalie said.

Jaque spoke with the waiter. "They'll bring in some trays of food and put them in the back," he said.

"Go ahead, Andrea," Natalie said.

Andrea was about to point to the next slide when Aysha came into the room. She looked around. "I'm not late, am I?" she asked.

"You're on time," Jaque said. "We are running behind schedule, though."

Aysha took a seat after fixing herself a plate of food.

"On the product side," Andrea said, "we've analyzed alternative pricing models for our current customers."

Shaine changed the slide.

"This would be a major price increase for our existing customers," Natalie said.

"We've also looked into scenarios where we offboard the customers for which we do more work than their current fees cover," Andrea said. "Offboarding 10% of the customers that need the most alterations to our systems would increase our profitability."

Natalie shifted in her seat. "You want to offboard customers," she said.

"Yes," Andrea said, "that's one scenario."

Natalie scoffed.

"I don't like it either," Jaque said. "My sales team fights tooth and nail to keep every customer. But the truth is we're bleeding money from some of our major accounts."

Natalie looked at her phone.

"We can also sell some of our minor products to our competitors," Andrea continued.

Shaine changed the slide.

"As you can see," Andrea said, "our products would complement many of our competitor's existing product suites."

"We haven't gauged interest yet," Shaine said, "for obvious reasons."

"But we have had several of our competitors indicate interest in those products," Jaque said. "Even last week, one of my sales reps had a conversation with a competitor at a trade fair."

Natalie stood up from her chair. "Many of these products predate ASLO," she said.

"You designed many of these products," Mark said.

Andrea looked around the room. "Shall we continue?" she asked.

"Go ahead," Jaque said.

Shaine changed the slide.

"Lastly," Andrea said, "we could sell ASLO itself. That would allow the new owners to re-host it and claim a different price, as well as stop the financial bleeding of the company entirely."

Shaine changed the slide.

"As you can see from this summary table," Andrea said, "most of these scenarios require some investment. An investment that won't be paid back until, in some cases, several years later."

"It's not just the data center you want to sell for parts," Natalie said. "You're essentially selling Zebra for parts."

"Now, don't shoot the messenger," Jaque said.

"We have printouts of this slide," Shaine said, "so that you can reference it while Aysha takes us through our financial situation."

The door opened slowly, and some conference center staff came in to wheel the lunch trays away. Marie realized that she hadn't eaten yet. She was about to flag down the staff to ask for a plate. But, as the wagons passed her, the cheese looked sweaty and melted. Marie's stomach churned, and she decided to skip lunch. Instead, she refocused on what was happening in the room. Natalie, the slide printout in hand, was arguing with Jaque. Richard was studying the numbers on the printout. Mark had turned his chair toward the window. Jenni was sipping a can of cola.

"Let's continue," said Aysha loudly, then clapped her hands.

Jaque came toward the front of the room.

"I know this is difficult," Jaque said, "but if we stand together, we can find a way forward from here."

"Let's see your numbers," Richard said.

Natalie sat down.

Aysha took a deep breath. "As you know, we have been struggling financially for months now," she said. She pointed the clicker toward the screen and changed slides. "If we do nothing and continue with our current customer load and assets, we won't make our salary payments in January."

She pointed to a graph showing monthly forecasts and different kinds of costs. "Based on projections that we keep losing customers as we have been in recent months, and assuming we're unable to onboard new ones, we may well find that we run out of funds as soon as October," Aysha said.

Marie's mouth opened. She hadn't realized how deep the company's financial troubles ran.

Jaque went to the front of the room again. "Now, I know this sounds bad," he said, "but if we implement one or several of the scenarios proposed, we can still turn this ship around."

"No, it's too late," Mark said. "All of these require investment." Mark pointed to the printout of the scenarios.

"They also require time," Richard said. "Finding buyers and agreeing contracts will take more than three months."

Natalie stood up, fists clenched, mouth shut. She looked around. "You are idiots," she shouted, "all of you. You've completely forgotten what this company is about. We were supposed to make teaching easier for teachers. Make learning easier for students. Instead, you're making slides and crunching numbers, plotting to take the company apart piece by piece."

She looked at Jenni. "You just stood by doing nothing while your engineers ran ASLO into the ground," she said through her teeth.

Jenni's eyes widened.

"You prance around like you own the place," she said, looking at Jaque.

"Now wait a minute ..." Jaque began, but Natalie gestured at him to stop.

"You try to mend every fence while forgetting why there are fences in the first place," she said to Marie.

Marie's mouth fell open, and she looked toward Mark. Mark's lips were tightly sealed.

"And you ..." she said, looking at Richard. "You left me when I needed you the most."

She looked around again. She took a deep breath and opened her mouth, but instead of saying anything, she walked straight toward the door, slamming it behind her as she left.

The door re-opened a few seconds afterward, and one of the conference center staff peeked in. "Are you guys ready for cake?" she asked.

Cakeless

Marie was pouring herself a cup of coffee. Her hands were still shaking from Natalie's comments. Jenni was eating a slice of red velvet cake. Jaque was on the phone. He had just sent Aysha, Andrea, and Shaine away. Richard spoke to Mark while keeping an eye on the door and shifting from one leg to another. He headed toward the door. Marie followed him with her eyes as she sat down next to Jenni.

"Some workshop," Jenni said. "It's all your fault, you know."

"What are you talking about?" Marie said.

"If you had let me run engineering my way," Jenni said, "we wouldn't be in this mess."

"Are you kidding me?" Marie said.

"Your HR voodoo has only made things worse," Jenni said.

"You had a mutiny on your hands," Marie shouted.

"Only because you insisted on accommodating their demands," Jenni said.

"I can't believe you," Marie said. "After everything, you blame me for your department being in disarray."

"I should never have trusted you," Jenni said.

"That's your takeaway from today?" Marie shouted. "That I've gotten in your way."

Mark approached Jenni and Marie with a stern look on his face. "Jenni," Mark said, "how about you and I take a walk?"

"I don't need a walk with more HR people," Jenni said.

"Then I suggest you walk away," Mark said.

Jenni looked at him. Then at Marie. She threw her plate on the chair next to her and got up to leave. "You're a bunch of bullshitters," she said. She grabbed her bag and stormed out of the room.

Jaque hung up his phone. "Where is Jenni off to?" he asked.

"She needed a minute," Mark said.

"What's the plan, Jaque?" Marie asked.

"We still have a decision to make," Jaque said, "otherwise we'll run out of money come October."

Marie's phone vibrated in the pocket of her blazer. It was Ally's school friend's mom. Marie looked at the time. It was 5:30 p.m. "Shit," Marie shouted. She grabbed her bag and sprinted for the door.

"What's wrong?" Mark shouted.

"I was supposed to pick up Ally from kindergarten," Marie shouted as she ran toward the exit.

Sitting in Carrie's mom's kitchen, Ally's face was covered in chocolate cake. The chocolate cake was homemade. So was the vanilla ice cream served with it. Marie kissed Ally on the forehead.

"Hi, Mommy," Ally said and kept working on her cake.

"Carrie and Ally have played well together," Carrie's mom said.

"Thank you for bringing Ally home with you," Marie said.

"My mother's intuition told me you might be late," Carrie's mom said, "so we stuck around until kindergarten closed."

"I really appreciate it," Marie said.

"Good thing we did, too," Carrie's mom went on. "You never showed."

"There's a lot going on at work right now," Marie said.

"Somehow, the rest of us manage to pick our kids up before closing," Carrie's mom said, "and some of us remember to bring sprinkles and decorations for events."

Marie looked at Carrie's mom in disbelief.

"I called Thomas too, you know," Carrie's mom continued. "He's on his way."

"Why would you call both of us?" Marie asked.

"I think it's time the two of you had a bit of a chat about your priorities," Carrie's mom said.

Marie got up from her chair. "Who do you think you are?" she said.

"I'm the mother who picks up your child when you forget," Carrie's mom said. "I'm an actual mother."

Marie was about to shout but looked at Ally's face and swallowed. Swallowed hard.

"Ally, honey, let's go home," Marie said, her voice breaking.

"I haven't finished my cake, Mommy," Ally said.

"I know, sweetie," Marie said. "You'll have to visit Carrie another time."

Ally took one last bite of cake and stood up. "Bye, Carrie," she said, waving to her friend.

Marie looked at Carrie's mom one more time. "Thank you for picking Ally up," she said sternly. "You are not to take my child without my consent again."

"Would you rather let the social authorities take her?" Carrie's mom said.

"I would rather let the kindergarten call her mother," Marie said. She bent down and helped Ally tie her shoes.

"Bye-bye," Ally said and waved at Carrie's mom.

"You be brave, honey," Carrie's mom said.

Marie looked back at Carrie's mom and slammed the door as hard as she could.

"That was loud," Ally said.

"That was very loud, honey," Marie said.

Ally was asleep when Thomas arrived. He had been at an offsite with his company. Marie was filling the dishwasher when he walked into the kitchen. She turned to kiss him, but he pulled away.

"Carrie's mom called," he said.

Marie rolled her eyes.

"How could you forget to pick up Ally?" Thomas said.

"We had an offsite at work," Marie said. "The company's in deep trouble."

"How can your work be more important than our daughter?" Thomas said.

"Are you kidding me right now?" Marie said. "You were also at a company offsite today."

"You've been completely absorbed by work this past year," Thomas said. "It's like an addiction for you."

"And you take your job lightly?" Marie said. "Never ruminating about your work problems when you're home?"

"It's not about that, Marie," he said. "Look at you; you've lost weight in the last few months." Thomas pulled out the waist of Marie's pencil skirt. Marie shook his hand off. "Have you eaten at all today?" he asked.

"Everyone is on my case," Marie shouted. "I eat, for crying out loud."

"Carrie's mom said you shouted at her," Thomas said.

Marie looked him straight in the face. "Did that woman call you again after I left?" she said.

"She called me three times today," Thomas said.

Marie's stomach sank. "How often does she usually call you?" Marie asked.

"I don't know," Thomas said, "a couple of times a week."

"And what does she want a couple of times a week?" Marie asked.

"I don't always pick up," Thomas said. He looked at Marie. "You're never here," he said. "You work late."

"And is Carrie's mom here?" Marie asked.

"What are you implying?" Thomas said.

Marie looked at him.

He sighed. "No, Carrie's mom is not here," he said. "I love you, Marie."

Marie rolled her eyes. "Why would she keep calling you if you don't pick up?" she said.

"I do pick up," Thomas said.

"You just said you didn't," Marie said.

"It's nice to have someone pay attention to me," Thomas said.

"I pay attention to you," Marie said.

"You barely do," Thomas said. "All we talk about is work or Ally. Or what's-his-name who you have coffee with from your competitor."

"Todd," Marie said.

"I bet you pay him more attention," Thomas said. He shrugged. "You're never here. And when you are, you're somewhere else. Now you're leaving Ally with strangers."

"Apparently, Carrie's mom is no stranger," Marie said.

"Stop it, Marie," Thomas said. "There's nothing there."

"There is clearly something," Marie said.

"I want you," Thomas said, "but do you even want to be here?"

Marie's phone rang. She let it finish ringing. Then it rang again, and she picked it up. Thomas shook his head and walked out of the kitchen. It was Jaque. Marie agreed to come back to the offsite. She left without saying a word to Thomas.

As Marie entered the meeting room, Jaque was speaking. Natalie, Mark, Richard, and Jason were huddled around a meeting chart. Richard was holding Natalie's shoulder.

"I think we have to investigate if ASLO can be sold off completely," Jaque said.

"Wow," Marie said, "I didn't see that coming."

Jaque waved for her to join them at the meeting chart. "I have a bit of an unorthodox idea," Jason said.

"Why are you here?" Marie asked, looking at Jason.

"I called him," Jaque said.

Marie shrugged.

"What's your idea?" Mark asked.

"While I was away from Zebra," Jason said, "I worked for the defense contractor. Even though it turned out not to be my cup of tea, I was right about the military being in transition when it comes to their approach to learning. The war in Ukraine is not just physical. It's as much a war of information. For example, there was a campaign recently about how the wife of Ukraine's president spent excessive amounts on jewelry. It turned out to be completely fake, but it almost deterred US Congress from providing additional aid."

"What does this have to do with learning?" Jaque asked.

"What the defense contractor actually does," Jason said, "is train counter-information officers to investigate and retaliate against such information campaigns. Since Russian tactics keep changing, the officers need to be retrained almost weekly. A full corps of trainers creates new curricula every week to ensure that the information officers can be effective."

"This sounds like a perfect use case for ASLO," Natalie said.

"I've wanted to contribute to the war effort ever since the war started," Jason said. "We tried to get Zebra to donate ASLO to the displaced children of Ukraine, but providing ASLO as a tool in the war effort would make a much bigger difference."

"Why wouldn't the defense contractor just become an ASLO user?" Jaque asked.

"They can't risk anyone else having access to their information," Jason said. "They would want to store ASLO on their own servers, inaccessible to the outside world."

"They would buy the whole platform," Marie said.

"Yes," Jason said, "and keep it confidential."

"We would have to offboard all our existing users," Natalie said.

"We're losing money on them anyway," Jaque said. "This way, we ingest capital into the system to be able to invest in the data center."

"Then the data center could be Zebra," Richard said.

"This would upend the whole company," Marie said.

"This way, there would still be a company," Jaque said.

When Marie snuck into their bedroom, Thomas was asleep. She quietly took her clothes off and lay next to him. She tried to cuddle him, but he brushed her arms away. It was 3 a.m.

A Shift In Learning

"I'd been fearing this day would come," Marie said, sitting across from Willie in the conference center. It was morning, and Marie was holding a cup of fresh coffee.

"Once Shaine let me know that he told you about my casting, I thought I might as well get it over with," Willie said.

"What role will you be playing?" Marie asked.

"I'll be playing a supporting part in a musical," Willie said.

"You never cease to amaze me, Willie," Marie said.

"It's not a big part," Willie said, "but it's enough to pay the bills." Willie looked around. "And it seems like this place is coming apart at the seams."

"I'm not sure it's falling apart so much as shape-shifting," she said.

"My last day will be the end of the month," he said.

They both looked at their coffees.

"What made you choose to pursue your passion now?" Marie asked.

"I made quite the impression with the sugar stunt," Willie said.

"That was a solid piece of performance art," Marie said.

"The biggest push was when I discovered you were considering discontinuing the data center," Willie said. "I'd worked so hard to make that data center the best it could be. I know every single piece of machinery in there."

Marie bit her lip.

"But I also asked myself, why am I investing so much in a career I never actually wanted?" Willie said. "What if I took the same chance on myself as Richard took on me?"

Marie smiled. "Seems like your bet has paid off," she said.

Marie was walking up the stairs to give Paul and Mark the news of Willie's resignation when she met Mark in the stairwell. "We have a resignation," Marie said.

"How did you hear about it already?" Mark asked.

"Willie just resigned," Marie said. "He has a part in a musical."

Mark smiled. "Good for him," Mark said, "he's always been a creative soul."

"Which resignation are you talking about?" Marie asked.

"Jenni's," Mark said. "She just resigned half an hour ago."

"Did she give a reason?" Marie asked.

"She just sent an email," Mark said. "No explanation."

"We can both guess that last week's workshop must have played a part," Marie said.

"The fact is she's resigning and has asked to be put on garden leave effective immediately," Mark said. "The question is, who could we assign to be head of engineering in the interim?"

"Lilly," Marie said.

"Not Ibrahim?" Mark said. "He's been here the longest."

"Lilly has the mind of a true leader," Marie said, "and is respected among the engineers."

"Sounds like a plan to me," Mark said. "I'll speak to Natalie."

"I'll speak to Lilly," Marie said.

Mark looked up the stairs. "I need to get up there," he said. "We've received an offer for ASLO from Jason's former employer."

On Thursday morning, Marie met Todd in the coffee shop. This time, Anne was sitting at the table with Todd when Marie arrived.

"I didn't know you were joining us, Anne," Marie said as she sat down.

"I asked Anne to come," Todd said. "Like you and me, Anne is a fellow traveler trying to make companies work."

Marie looked at Anne.

"I'm closing my consulting practice," Anne said. "I'll be joining Jason's former company."

"You'll be working for a defense contractor?" Marie asked.

"It seems they may be in need of my specific product expertise," Anne said.

Marie nodded.

"Seems like we might be able to make a difference to the war effort after all," Anne said.

"Wait a minute," Marie said, "I thought you enjoyed advising companies on how to make their work more efficient?"

Anne looked down. "I don't think any of us really knows what makes companies work better," she said. "All we can do is stay in the struggle."

"What do you mean?" Marie said. "You've been giving me advice about what to do at Zebra Apps ever since you left."

"I left things unresolved," Anne said. "I did what I could at Zebra, but I ran out of moves."

Marie shook her head. "I was a pawn that gave you more moves at Zebra," Marie countered.

"I wouldn't put it quite like that," Anne said.

"How would you put it?" Marie asked.

"Marie," Anne said, "you managed to do more for Zebra's organizational development than I ever did. Your power base was anchored more strongly."

"This is bullshit, Anne," Marie said. "Here I was listening to your advice, and all you were trying to do was clear your conscience."

"I was sharing what I knew," Anne said.

"You clearly knew nothing," Marie said. "I trusted you."

"You *can* trust me," Anne contested.

"I can trust you to linger," Marie said.

"I helped you maneuver," Anne said.

"Your maneuvers did nothing for ASLO," Marie said.

"Now I *will* be able to do something about ASLO," Anne said.

Todd looked at Anne and Marie. "The three of us try our best to create great organizations," Todd said.

"Sometimes we fail," Anne said.

"At least now you can fail with your own ass on the line," Marie retorted.

"My ass can take a beating," Anne said.

"I think mine is down for the count," Marie said.

Anne chuckled. Marie smiled carefully.

Jaque had invited Marie out to dinner that evening. Just the two of them. This led to another fight with Thomas.

"The deal for ASLO's takeover has been signed," Jaque confirmed.

"That was fast," Marie said.

"We're going to launch a press release in the coming week," Jaque said.

"What will we do with our existing customers?" Marie asked.

"Natalie and Jason have devised an alternative solution for them using one of our older applications," Jaque said.

"They'll sell them an alternative?" Marie asked.

"Actually, Natalie decided to persuade the schools that use our solution to form a co-op," Jaque answered, "so that they'll own and invest in the development of the product without making a profit."

"This sounds like one of Jason's ideas," Marie said.

"I'm not sure," Jaque said, "but Natalie is very excited about it."

Marie looked at Jaque. "She seems happier focusing on making the lives of teachers and students easier than on building a profitable company," she said.

"I would say she's found her passion again," Jaque said.

Marie nodded.

"How do you feel about building a profitable company?" Jaque asked.

"I feel good about it," Marie said.

"You've done a good job analyzing and figuring out how to make our engineering department work and how to get from our many problems to actual solutions," Jaque praised.

Marie sighed. "It wasn't much use, though," she said. "It was too late."

"That doesn't discredit your work," Jaque said.

"Perhaps not," Marie said.

"With the sale of ASLO, we'll have enough capital to make an initial investment in the co-op for our existing customers," Jaque said, "but we'll also have sufficient funds to spin out the data center as an AI learning company."

"I see," Marie said, "so we can utilize the data center for what it was actually built for."

Jaque nodded. "I'll become the CEO of the AI learning company," Jaque said.

"Of course you will," Marie said.

"Richard and Natalie will be on the board," Jaque continued, "and I'm fighting tooth and nail to convince Aysha to head up the finance team."

"Seems like I'm out of a job," Marie said.

Jaque smiled. "I want you to join as my COO," he said.

"What?" Marie said.

Jaque nodded. "It would entail you building this company with me," he said, "for the benefit of our users but also for profit."

"I …" Marie stuttered. "What about all the people at Zebra? Where are they going to be employed?"

"Your first job will be to put your team together," Jaque said. "The team should be able to define the product and the pricing structure for the product."

Marie looked down. "I've had my ass handed to me trying to save Zebra," she said. "It might have cost me my marriage. I'm not sure I'm cut out for this."

Jaque leaned toward her. "What you do best is listen to the people who already know what to do," Jaque said. "You take them seriously and give them a voice. I need the company to have a people champion. You're my champion. I want the names of your team on my desk on Monday."

The New Mission

Jason cut the cake and passed plates around. He handed a plate to Marie. "Thank you so much for coming," he exclaimed.

She spotted Natalie in the crowd and nodded at her. Natalie was surrounded by chatting people.

"Hey, Marie," Anne said, also holding a piece of cake.

Marie hugged Anne with one arm. "Quite the turnout for the launch of Teaching United," she said.

"They've done a good job converting most ASLO customers to the new co-op platform," Anne said.

"Have you seen it?" Marie asked.

"I haven't," Anne said, "but I'm sure it's a great product. Lilly is an amazing engineer, and I can't believe they convinced both Tom and Dennis to join the development team."

"Yeah, that was a big pay cut for them," Marie said.

"For some people, the mission is more important than the pay package," Anne said.

"And how is your product doing?" Marie asked.

"I've been very lucky to get Ibrahim and Drue on the team," Anne said. She leaned in closer to Marie. "It's not in good shape, though. At this point, we might need to rewrite the entire code base."

"Fingers crossed that it makes it out of the woods," Marie said.

Anne nodded.

"How is Jo doing?" Marie asked. "I don't see her tonight."

"She's amazing," Anne said. "She has such a cool head for designing training programs."

Anne looked at Marie. "How is it working with Simon and Shaine?" she asked. "I was surprised that you picked them for your team."

"They fight on every occasion," Marie said, "but at least that surfaces all the issues, and we have ample fresh ideas."

"Hello, ladies," Eric said, also holding some cake.

"Eric!" Marie exclaimed and hugged him.

"Careful now," Eric said, "I don't want to drop Paul's cake."

"No way," Marie said. "Did Paul make this?"

"He's a baker now," Eric said. "He enjoys managing his baking business as much as the actual baking."

"I miss working with you guys," Marie said.

Eric put a hand on Marie's shoulder. "Have you seen Willie's musical yet?" he asked.

"I've seen it," Anne said. "He's phenomenal. I had no idea he could sing like that."

"I have tickets for this weekend," Eric said, "so no spoilers."

Eric pulled Marie closer to him. "How are you and Thomas?" he asked.

"We've pulled through," Marie said. "It wasn't just about my work. It was also the expectation he had that I pull most of the weight at home while also working."

"The curse of the modern woman who is supposed to do it all," Anne said.

Marie hugged Jason goodbye after hearing all about the new co-op and how the development of the new platform for learning had been democratized. She was heading toward her car in the parking lot when she saw Mark walking toward her.

"Mark!" she shouted. Mark waved at her. They sat down in Marie's car. "I haven't seen you in months," Marie said. "What have you been up to?"

"You know," Mark said, "not much really." Marie looked at him. "I felt like I had lost my way at Zebra," Mark continued. "I was so focused on coaching Natalie and making sure that she became the CEO we needed that I never stepped back to consider whether that was worth doing." He sighed. "Clearly, it wasn't. She's much happier now working directly with teachers and students on designing a product that makes sense to them."

"I don't think you could have known that," Marie said.

"And I never saw that Jaque had the potential to become a CEO," Mark said.

Marie laughed. "To be clear," Marie said, "Jaque is still a pain in the ass."

Mark smiled. "I bet he is," he said, "but a competent one. One who doesn't stop when things are difficult or decisions need to be made."

"You've been a good boss to me," she said.

Mark shook his head. "You and I both know that's the modified truth," he said. "I need to take some time to figure out what I want."

"That's fair," Marie said.

"I'm sleeping a lot these days," Mark said.

"That's good," Marie said.

"Or maybe it's a sign of depression," Mark said.

"Maybe it's a sign that you've been putting off rest," Marie said.

"Regardless, it's the phase I'm in," Mark said.

Marie sighed. "Even though I'm excited to be part of Zebra AI now and that I got to pick my own team," Marie said, "I keep doubting my own influence. Does the work I do even matter?"

"You've always assumed that you need to have control," Mark said, "but your influence never came from control. It came from listening to the experts and bringing their thinking together."

Acknowledgments

The storyline of this book was developed as an experiment. We started with the first chapter in 2022. We wanted to take an alternative approach to writing a book and to involve competent and passionate people in the process, so we invented the *Maneuvering Monday* podcast. We wrote one chapter at a time, published it as an audiobook with 3–4 sections, and invited guest experts to comment on Marie's challenges at Zebra Apps. The idea was to learn from our guest experts' maneuvers and let their input guide the progression of the storyline. We want to acknowledge all the minds and hearts that helped us realize our project.

Thank you to Tiffany Lam, Katie Christensen, and Ben Balassa for narrating our story in the story parts of the *Maneuvering Monday* podcast. You enabled our project and we could not have done it without you.

Thank you to all our wonderful guest experts from the commentary episodes of the *Maneuvering Monday* podcast: Claus Vagner, Puk Falkenberg, Patrick Sheridan, Anne Weber Carlsen, Benoit Hurel, Sam McAfee, Heidi Helfand, Dr. Ross Wirth, Christian Feldbech Nissen, Dr. Cherry Vu, Rob England, Març-Peter Pijper, Vivek Menon, Joe Auslander, Laurence Paquette, Mary Lemmer, David Billouz, Michelle Leedy, Paul Hargreaves, Katja Schipperheijn, Sofie Henriksen, and Cecil "Gary" Rupp. You all helped form Marie's story and we are grateful that we got to spend time with each of you and learn from your experiences.

Thank you to our great beta readers, Christian Feldbech Nissen, Joe Auslander, Simon Rosendal, and Dimitri Borisevich, who helped us prepare the final manuscript of the book for publication.

Finally, we want to thank our families for relentlessly supporting our project, listening, reading, asking, and cheering us on from start to end. Kenneth, Anna, Kamma, Ada, and Akira—this book would not have seen the light of day without you.

The Authors

Ivanna Mikhailovna Rosendal

Born in 1987 in eastern Ukraine, Ivanna grew up amidst the instability of the post-Soviet collapse, which taught her the importance of adapting and seeking better ways to do things. Witnessing the stark contrast between the lives of two friends' fathers who worked in different coal mines—one exploited and hopeless, the other valued and happy—instilled a passion for creating dignified workplaces. This led her to a career in behavioral economics and life sciences. Now, as the VP of Digitalization for a biotech, she focuses on leveraging technology to enhance the work of scientists and medical teams, ensuring they can make an impact on patient outcomes. Through initiatives like the podcast *Transformations in Trials,* she aims to make life sciences more accessible and foster collaboration to drive meaningful change. She believes art can speak truth when every other voice is silenced, which is why she has written and directed a short film, *The Other Side,* about the impact of war in families with both Ukrainian and Russian roots. The storytelling techniques in this book are born out of Ivanna's passion for improvisational theater and comedy.

www.linkedin.com/in/ivannarosendal

Anne Katrine Carlsson Sejr

As a leader of teams specializing in organizational development and transformation, AK has often been frustrated by the oversimplified advice in business literature. She therefore set out to write a story that feels real—where leaders don't have all the answers, mistakes happen, and the best intentions still meet resistance. While launching this project, she has been on a personal journey, having her first child when the podcast was born and expecting her second as the book is released. The project has been both a creative outlet and a way to shape a story that her daughters might one day read and be inspired by.

AK believes work takes up too much of our lives to be miserable, and *Maneuvering Monday* is for anyone trying to make work better, one imperfect step at a time.

www.linkedin.com/in/anne-katrine-carlsson-sejr-890a04108

Maneuvering Monday

Together, Ivanna and AK host the *Maneuvering Monday* podcast, where experts and thought leaders share insights, experiences, and concrete maneuvers to tackle the challenges inspired by the book's main characters and dilemmas.

https://maneuveringmonday.buzzsprout.com